Christian
Morality
Today

Fides Publishers, Inc., Notre Dame, Ind.

Christian
Morality
Today

Charles E. Curran

BJ
1249
C8

0 11645

The Renewal of Moral Theology

Contents

Moral Theology in the Light of Vatican II

Preface

The nine chapters of this book were originally written during the past three years in response to requests for a moral and theological consideration of particular topics. Although this volume makes no attempt at a systematic presentation of moral theology, many of the pressing problems of moral theology are discussed: conscience, freedom, natural law, birth control, mixed marriages. The unifying element in the book is the *aggiornamento*, the renewal of moral theology—the same spirit of renewal which in general has characterized the Vatican Council. Naturally there are particular points and emphases that I would express differently today, but the basic approach and essential thrust of the chapters faithfully represents my current thinking. For the most part, I have resisted the temptation to make any changes in the original papers. The discerning reader will note the development in my own thinking on certain points.

Perhaps the most noticeable lack in the book is a more communitarian consideration of the Christian life. The theological and liturgical emphases on the Christian community and the corporate Christian personality find a resonant chord in the awareness of modern man of belonging to the whole human community. This volume reminds me in a very forceful manner of my communion with and dependence on so many other people. Briefly, I wish to thank all those from whom I have learned so much—my parents, family, friends, colleagues, teachers—especially Fr. Bernard Häring, C.SS.R., and my students—particularly those from St. Bernard's Seminary in Rochester, New York. Mr. Eugene S. Geissler was instrumental in suggesting the present volume and most helpful in its publication.

Grateful acknowledgment is made to the following publishers for permission to reprint certain chapters in this book:

Guide, for THE RENEWAL OF THEOLOGY; The Belknap Press of Harvard University Press, for THE CHRISTIAN CONSCIENCE TODAY, © 1964 by the President and Fellows of Harvard College; The Society of Catholic College Teachers of Sacred Doctrine, for FORMATION IN FREEDOM AND RESPONSIBILITY; *Jubilee,* for CHRISTIAN MARRIAGE AND FAMILY PLANNING; *The Current,* for PERSONAL REFLECTIONS ON BIRTH CONTROL; *The Lamp,* for NATURAL LAW AND THE TEACHING AUTHORITY OF THE CHURCH; *The Jurist,* for THE MIXED MARRIAGE PROMISES; The National Council of Catholic Men, for CATHOLIC CONVICTIONS ON SUNDAY OBSERVANCE; The Liturgical Conference, for THE RELEVANCE OF MORAL THEOLOGY TODAY, in *Jesus Christ Reforms His Church* (Washington, D. C., The Liturgical Conference, 1965).

Introduction

Vatican II has issued no decree or constitution on moral theology. Yet the *aggiornamento* which has characterized the ecumenical council must also renew the science of moral theology. For the most part the present textbooks and manuals of moral theology have now become obsolete—not because they are in error, but because they are not in keeping with the whole spirit of renewal in the Church today. The Council has not left us a blueprint for the future textbooks of moral theology, but the spirit of the Vatican Council has established the broad outlines for the further development of moral theology.

THE ORIENTATION OF MORAL THEOLOGY

For the most part, the textbooks of moral theology have pursued the rather limited aim of training confessors; and even then, the textbooks pay little attention to the role of the confessor as father, teacher, and physician. In our contemporary situation should moral theology have the rather narrow scope of merely training confessors as judges? Whatever the reason might be, most of our people today know what is sinful; and in confession they are looking more for the consolation and advice they need to live better their daily lives as Christians. Even with regard to the narrow purposes of training confessors as judges, the textbooks no longer fulfill their intended function. The real problems for the confessor concern the existence of subjective sin in the particular penitent here and now. Very frequently the confessor can only leave the matter in the merciful hands of God. Contemporary critics, however, should not totally condemn the existing manuals of moral theology. The origin of our present textbooks represents a marvelous *aggiornamento*, a true accommodation to the needs and spirit of a given time. The renewal of the Christian life and the sacrament of penance in the sixteenth century after the Council of Trent called for priests to be trained as confessors. The *Institutiones Theologiae Moralis*, the forerunners of our present textbooks, represented a successful crash program for the training of confessors. But the same needs and historical circumstances do not exist today.

Moral theology, with such a narrow scope, necessarily concentrated on the minimal, the dividing line between mortal and venial sin. Even such negative considerations reflected the humane and benign attitude of not imposing on Christians anything more than was required. Despite a clumsy and very juridical approach, the older moralists tried to safeguard the freedom of the children of God. Moral theology also reflected the defensive and protective attitude that characterized Catholic life for the last few centuries—the ghetto mentality. If reference is made to the world in any moral treatises, the reference often occurs solely under the heading of "occasions of sin." The good Catholic tried to defend and protect his faith against the incursions of the world. Catholic thought created a false dichotomy between matter and spirit, body and soul, which is completely foreign to biblical thought. Catholic spirituality implied that man recharged his spiritual life through the performance of certain spiritual exercises, but in daily contact with the world man's spiritual battery wore down. If life in the world was not incompatible with holiness and perfection, at least living in the world was not the perfect or better way of serving God. In such a light one can easily see how the gulf developed between the spiritual life of man and his daily existence in our society and world. Emphasis was placed on certain actions (e.g., Friday abstinence) and practices (e.g., novenas, candles) that soon became irrelevant for many people precisely because they bore no real meaning for daily life.

A legalistic and rationalistic attitude, combined with a defensive posture, saw Christian morality in the light of a conformity with pre-existing laws and structures. Every action involved the fear of sin and going against the established order. The passive virtues of loyalty, docility, and obedience became the great Christian attitudes. The closed concept of morality looked down on everything new as suspect and a threat to the existing structures. Perhaps some of the above remarks are overly severe, but such attitudes definitely colored the orientation of moral theology.

The spirit of Vatican II and the needs of our own time must influence the orientation of moral theology today. A life centered moral theology should replace the confessional oriented approach of the older textbooks. The *Constitution on the Church* in Chapter V boldly proclaims the universal vocation of all Christians to holiness. "Thus it is evident to everyone that all the faithful of Christ of whatever rank or status are called to the fullness of the Christian life and to the perfection of charity" (¶ 40). Moral theology needs to show how the Christian pursues his vocation to holiness in the modern world.

The attitude of moral theology can no longer be minimal and defensive. The *Constitution on the Church in the Modern World* acknowledges: "The split between the faith which many profess and their daily lives deserves to be counted among the more serious errors of our age" (¶ 43). The Christian life implies a service to humanity and the world—"that we may build a better world based on truth and justice." The Council clearly indicates that the moral and spiritual life of the Christian in the world requires a working for the cultural, economic, social, and political good of humanity. The Christian vocation in the world calls for the elimination of all human misery which is incompatible with the dignity of the human person so frequently mentioned in conciliar documents. The *Decree on the Apostolate of the Laity* develops the key theme that "the Christian vocation by its very nature is also a vocation to the apostolate" (¶ 2). The second Vatican Council has sounded the death knell for a moral theology that is primarily confession oriented, minimalistic and individualistic.

Likewise, moral theology can no longer emphasize conformity to rigid and static laws as if everything were completely spelled out in pre-existing norms. The Council insists that the Christian continue the creative and redemptive work of God in the world. The Christian life receives its dynamism from a sharing in the mission and role of Christ: "Clearly then a great promise and a great trust is committed to the disciples: 'All things are yours, and you are Christ's and Christ is God's'" (I Cor 3:23) (*Constitution on the Church*, ¶ 36). The final exhortation in the *Decree on the Apostolate of the Laity* reads: "The most holy Council then earnestly entreats all the laity in the Lord to answer gladly, nobly, and promptly the more urgent invitation of Christ . . . to associate themselves with him in his saving mission. Once again he sends them into every town and place where he will come so that they may show that they are co-workers in the various forms and modes of the one apostolate of the Church, which must be constantly adapted to the new needs of our times." The Christian mission and apostolate reflect the dynamic continuing mission of Christ and remain always open to approaches and structures that are more adapted to the changing circumstances of our times.

Growth and dynamism characterize not only the Christian mission but the Christian life itself. The call of all men to perfection means that the Christian life is a continual conversion. The conciliar documents frequently mention the pilgrim Church, but what is said of the Church also applies to the individual Christian. The Christian continues to grow closer to that perfect union with God and neighbor which will be achieved only in the future. Since growth and dynamism characterize both the life and the mission of the Christian, creativity and not conformity needs to receive more emphasis. The Christian frequently must assume the risk of action and growth. Mere passivity or even conformity betrays the meaning of the Christian life. Contemporary moral theology should remind Christians of the parable of the master who left a sum of money for his servants. The master richly rewarded the servants who used the money to make more money, but the master severely condemned the servant who took the money and buried it in a field because he was afraid of losing it.

KEY EMPHASES IN MORAL THEOLOGY

SACRED SCRIPTURE. The second Vatican Council has tried to renew the central place of the scriptures in the life and theology of the Church. Unfortunately, the present text-books do not derive their format and inspiration from the Word of God. In treating particular moral questions, the existing textbooks generally follow a systematization either according to the cardinal and moral virtues or according to the ten commandments. The cardinal virtues are not Christian in origin, nor do they represent the more important Christian attitudes. For example, the scriptures place great stress on humility as the virtue of the poor of God and the necessary disposition to receive the saving love of God; but one very commonly used textbook disposes of humility in one short paragraph. Also the ten commandments, especially when wrenched out of the covenant context, do not reflect the meaning of the new life that Christ has brought to us. From the point of view of teaching ethical conduct, the Boy Scout oath might be better, for the Scout oath at least uses a positive formulation. Likewise, the considerations of fundamental moral theology or *De Principiis* do not mirror the scriptural approach to the meaning of the Christian life.

The *Constitution on Divine Revelation* shows the primacy of the gospel as "the source of all saving truth and moral teaching" (¶ 7) . "Sacred theology rests on the written word of God, together with sacred tradition, as its primary and perpetual foundation. By scrutinizing in the light of faith all truths stored up in the mystery of Christ, theology is most powerfully strengthened and constantly rejuvenated by that word. For the sacred scriptures contain the word of God and, since they are inspired, really are the word of God; and so the study of the sacred page is, as it were, the soul of sacred theology" (¶ 24) . To think that an exclusively biblical approach would solve all the problems confronting moral theology is a gross oversimplification; but moral theology should receive its inspiration, format, and content primarily from the Word of God.

CONSCIENCE. Moral theology can no longer be considered especially in the light of conformity of conduct with external norms or laws. In many ways the Council teaches that man must find the reason for his moral activity in the depths of his own person, in his conscience. <u>The moral life of the Christian consists in the development of his own Christian personality</u>. The *Declaration on Christian Education* states: "For a true education aims at the formation of the human person. . . . This sacred synod likewise declares that children and young people have a right to be motivated to appraise moral values with a right conscience, to embrace them with a personal adherence, together with a deeper knowledge and love of God" (¶ 1).

The *Declaration on Religious Liberty* teaches that man must respond to the call of God in the depths of his own person. The Council does not intend to deny any objectivity, but rather the very objectivity of the human person demands that he freely respond to the call of God in the depths of his own person. The moral life of the Christian, or any human being, springs from the inner core of his own personality. The Church never will and never can deny its teaching mission, but the Church's moral teaching always proposes what is the true development and growth of the Christian person. Because we are Christians we must act in such a manner.

HOLY SPIRIT. Above all the Council has underlined the role of the Holy Spirit as the source of all life and renewal in the Church. The Spirit sanctifies the Church and guides it through the hierarchical and charismatic gifts. He is the life-giving Spirit through whom we receive the life of God. The Spirit dwells in the hearts of the just and there he prays for us and bears witness to the fact that we are the sons of God (see *Constitution on the Church*, ¶ 4). Chapter Five of the *Constitution on the Church* declares that the Holy Spirit produces the holiness of the Church and its members. "Indeed he sent the Holy Spirit upon all men that he might move them inwardly to love God with their whole soul, with all their mind and all their strength (Mark 12:30) and that they might love each other as Christ loves them (see John 3:34; 15:12)" (¶ 40). Moral theology should center on the loving dialogue of the Christian with the Holy Spirit who unites us in love with the Father and with all men. The Christian must learn to discover and respond to the true inspiration of the Spirit who dwells in our hearts. The Christian life truly is the spiritual life—for the Spirit becomes both the source and the guiding force of the Christian life. The Spirit makes us the adopted sons of the Father, and the Spirit teaches and urges us to act as the sons of the Father. In many places the conciliar documents stress love as the primary obligation of the Christian. But Paul reminds us that the Spirit pours out the love of Christ into our hearts (Rom 5:5).

LITURGY. The conciliar emphasis on the liturgy likewise indicates that the moral life of the Christian implies the living out of the new life received in the sacramental encounter with the risen Christ in the Church. Authentic Christian actions are those which are developed from the life we as Christians have received. The importance of conscience, the Holy Spirit, and the liturgy in Christian morality shows that morality is intrinsic and not extrinsic; that is, good actions are those that develop from the very being of the person and not just those actions that are in conformity with external norms.

A more intrinsic approach to morality will also avoid the pitfall of dividing the moral life into isolated actions which are seen merely in their relationship to an external law and not to the total personality. For example, preachers and teachers occasionally mention the one mortal sin which will send a person straight to hell no matter how many other good things he has done in his life. But mortal sin can never be just one isolated action. Since mortal sin involves the total orientation of the person, the laws of human psychology remind us that man does not ordinarily make such a drastic change by just one isolated action. Rather the change begins to occur gradually in the person through a number of smaller and less important actions. The theologian must view the moral life with all its continuity and not merely as a collection of individual actions which are judged primarily according to extrinsic norms. Yes, individual actions are important, but such actions have a meaning only insofar as they express and at the same time make more profound the fundamental orientation of the person.

Consequently, a true moral formation does not consist primarily in learning certain rules of moral conduct. Moral formation means that the person learns from his own experience the authentic demands of being a Christian in the present world. Formation attempts to make the individual a more genuine person, for by living a truly Christian existence the Christian will know what is being asked of him in his daily life.

COMMUNITY. The documents on the Church, the liturgy, and the Church in the modern world emphasize the communitarian aspect of the Christian life. Heretofore moral considerations have been primarily individualistic—what must I do to save my soul? The main documents of the Council remind us of our corporate personality, the people of God, in pilgrimage toward the new heaven and the new earth. All must work together in truth and love to build up the body of Christ and bring all men and all creation into the unity and holiness of God.

FURTHER ATTITUDES

In keeping with the spirit of the Council moral theology must acquire some further attitudes. The theologian too is always trying to listen to the voice of the Spirit. However, moral theologians can never forget that the Spirit also speaks in the lives of Christians and all men of good will. The *Declaration on Religious Liberty* calls attention to the manifestations of the Spirit in the desires and witness of men. With regard to religious liberty the document says: "This Vatican Council takes careful note of these desires in the minds of men. It proposes to declare them to be greatly in accord with truth and justice. To this end it searches into the sacred tradition and doctrine of the Church—the treasury out of which the Church continually brings forth new things that are in harmony with the things that are old" (¶ 1). The *Constitution on the Church* also calls attention to the prophetic office in the Church (¶ 12). The Spirit also speaks in the lives of the Christian in whose hearts he dwells as well as in the lives of all men of good will. The theologian must always listen to the Spirit wherever he speaks.

Too often in the past moral theology has approached the question of conscience and determining what is right or wrong from too cerebral or rationalistic a viewpoint. Scripture, on the other hand, frequently mentions knowledge of God in conjunction with the love of God as part of an authentic experience of God. In its teaching magisterium the Church does not usually proceed in a purely rationalistic and *a priori* reasoning process. For example, the Church has condemned masturbation, but to the present day theologians cannot agree on the precise reason why masturbation is wrong. How does the Church know, how does the individual Christian know what is right or wrong? The revealed word of God and the Holy Spirit guide both the Church and the Christian. The Church as the community of the saved realizes from the lived experience of its members what is in conformity with the demands of Christian living. The term, conscience, indicates that our knowledge also comes from the lived experience of others. Certainly, the Church and the individual Christian must use their reason to find out the good, but the knowledge of good and evil goes far beyond a mere cerebral and rationalistic approach.

The *Constitution on the Church in the Modern World* acknowledges the complexity of the modern world. The Church and moral theology do not have all the answers to the problems presented by our contemporary society. The Council underscores the need for a true dialogue (not just a one-way conversation as if we had all the answers to tell others) with Protestants, non-Christians, and the world itself. In humble cooperation with all men of good will the Church and theology will better learn what God is doing in this world to bring all creation to its fulfillment. Moral theology needs to enter such a dialogue especially with the important sciences of our day (e.g., sociology, psychology, anthropology, etc.) which provide so many helpful insights into the meaning of man and the world.

Moral theology does not generally treat the question of punishment and hell. However, in the present circumstances perhaps moralists should give more consideration to the way morality is taught on a popular level. Too often teachers instill morality through fear. The Church can never deny or gloss over the teaching on hell, but all things belong in their proper perspective. The Christian life is above all the loving response to the saving love of God in Christ. Christian teaching always proposes the gospel—the good news of salvation. In regard to the future, moral teachers should follow the example of Chapter VII of the *Constitution on the Church*, the eschatological nature of the pilgrim Church, which so clearly indicates the only true destiny of the Church and the Christian. The Christian is called to that perfect union of love with God and neighbor which will be ours in heaven.

Pope Paul has stressed that *aggiornamento* does not mean a break with the true tradition of the past (cf., speech of

Pope Paul to the Council on Nov. 18, 1965). To discern the true tradition of the Church is one of the huge tasks confronting moral theology. Only exacting and scholarly historical studies can separate the true tradition of the Church from the historical and cultural overtones of a particular period and society. Moral theology in general has been very slow in investigating the historical backgrounds of the teaching of the Church on particular matters. Unfortunately, many primary texts are still unedited. The work of historical research is slow and tedious but absolutely necessary for a true understanding of the traditional teaching of the Church.

Renewal has become a slogan and even a battle cry in the Church today. However, as the Pope and the Council have constantly reminded us, renewal must begin especially in our own lives as Christians. A renewed or new moral theology aims above all at forming better Christians. No book or manual can ever make us better Christians, but they can serve to make us more aware of the redeeming love of Christ and more open to cooperate in bringing mankind and all creation to their eschatological fulfillment.

The Renewal
of Theology

Chapter One

"Me-too-ism" is a danger in any authoritarian teaching. It is a perennial danger for theology. "Triumphalism" is a similar danger. Theology has all the answers; there are no problems. Smugness and self-satisfaction are the consequences of triumphalism. "Sterile intellectualism" likewise constitutes a perpetual temptation and danger for theology. Ever since gnosticism, the flight from reality has tempted Christians. Unfortunately, in the past few centuries theology has not completely avoided such pitfalls. A sterile and mechanical repetition of what the previous generation said has often stifled growth and vitality.

Theology cannot rest on its laurels. Theology will never be perfect; it will never have all the answers. Theology, like man himself, like the Church, is on a pilgrimage—looking forward to the day when it will evaporate in the mystery of God, seen and lived face to face. But how can theology change? How can theology be vital?

The function of theology is to make the eternal Word of God present in the flesh and bone of present day reality. To speak to the people of our day in a language they can understand is not a false accommodation to the spirit of the world. Rather, it is a concrete extension of the Incarnation: the Word of God made incarnate to the people of the twentieth century just as the Word himself was made flesh in the given historical situation of two thousand years ago.

As worshipers in spirit and truth, theologians must penetrate ever more deeply the revealed Word of God. The Church itself over the years gradually comes to a clearer knowledge and understanding of the truths of revelation. Both dogma and theology under the inspiration of the Spirit through the work of men evolve and develop. (Some people willingly accept the development of theology as an historical fact, but they act as if the development stopped 50 years ago.)

To be in constant dialogue with the revealed Word of God and with the concrete circumstances of our present existence is the vital principle of all theological renewal. The Second Vatican Council illustrates the fundamental principle of renewal. The addresses of John XXIII and Paul VI constantly repeat the same refrain. Theology, like the individual Christian, like the Church itself, is constantly in a state of renewal.

Having stated the basic principle of all theological renewal, we will consider three influences that have particular importance in the present day renewal of theology. The most important aspect is the return to the scriptures and the Fathers of the Church. A second factor is the absence of a polemic or apologetic purpose. The third influence is a more personalist approach to man's relationship with God and his fellow men.

THE LACK OF A POLEMIC MOTIVE

Let us consider first the lack of a polemic motive in present day theological investigation. The theology of the past four centuries has been justly characterized as counter-Reformation theology. Counter-Reformation theology is not necessarily a pejorative term. In fact, it is an excellent illustration of the truly incarnational character of theology in dialogue with its own times.

After the Reformation, Catholic theology naturally stressed the aspects of Catholic thought which the Reformers denied. Like any reaction, there was the tendency to stress the elements of disagreement and to pass over lightly the vast areas of agreement. Unfortunately, subsequent generations mistook such a theology for a complete picture of revelation. Perhaps an illustration will clarify the thought. After a very young child is burned by touching a hot stove, the mother immediately warns the child never to touch the stove again. As the child grows older, however, the mother teaches her to distinguish between a hot and cold stove, to handle hot pots and pans, and even to turn on the stove. Likewise, counter-Reformation theology in the beginning can be justified at least on disciplinary grounds; but as a maturity developed, a more balanced view should have appeared. It is only now that a more balanced and mature viewpoint asserts itself.

For example, the Protestant Churches minimized or denied the sacramental system. Protestants, instead, strongly emphasized the Word of God as read in the scriptures and proclaimed in the pulpit. Catholic theology strenuously defended the sacraments but said little or nothing about the Word of God. It was not a part of the dispute. However, in subsequent generations the Word of God became a forgotten truth.

Today Catholic thought is again conscious of the primary

place and power of the Word of God. The scriptural renewal is proof. Likewise, the reading of the Word of God in the liturgy has taken on added importance. We speak of the sacramental or quasi-sacramental nature of the Word of God. God communicates himself to us in a very special way in his Word. Volumes are now being written on the theology of preaching and the proclaiming of the Word of God. Yet the textbooks being used in our colleges and seminaries do not even contain a treatise or consideration on the Word of God.

The entire treatise on the Church, ecclesiology, is a product of counter-Reformation theology. The reformers denied the visible element of the Church. Catholic theology then developed its whole discussion along the lines of proving the visible element in the Church. Nothing was said about the invisible element, the bond of faith and love uniting all the baptized in the family of God. Protestantism denied especially the primacy of the pope. The theological consideration of the Church as it exists in most textbooks of our times could better be termed a treatise on the primacy of the pope and not a treatise on the Church as such. The aim of the generally accepted consideration of the Church is purely apologetic—to show that the Roman Catholic Church under the pope is the true Church of Christ.

How different is the document on the Church promulgated by the Fathers of Vatican II! They proclaim in the very beginning that the Church is a mystery—the community of men joined by faith and love through Christ the Lord in the family of God the Father. The Church is the people of God, the bride of Christ, the body of Christ with all its members. Every member of the Church has his own function and part to play in building up the body of Christ. Hierarchy, as a particular function, is to be exercised for the good of the whole body. The members of the hierarchy are servants in the house of the Lord. The hierarchy and the priesthood are the visible manifestation on earth of the loving care of the head for the body. There will be no need for participated hierarchy or priesthood once the head and the body are perfectly united in heaven.

A MORE PERSONALIST APPROACH

The second influence in the present renewal of theology is a more personal concept of man's relationship with God. Existential philosophy and experimental psychology show man as a person striving to develop himself in relation to the "thou" of God and his neighbor. Present personalist trends in modern theological thought correspond to the biblical description of reality.

A typical example of a more personalist approach is evident in the theology of grace. Generally we think of grace as something that is received into the soul. What is the soul? I think everyone has his own picture of what the soul is—a miniature me, a heart shaped vessel, a round vase. Grace is something like water poured into this container. Grace is a thing received in the soul. We speak of a sin as a stain on the soul. But grace wipes away the stain of sin. If a person dies with the stain of sin on his soul he goes to hell. (It is my opinion that contemporary preaching and teaching should avoid, if possible, using the word soul. Soul has a distorted meaning for most Catholics. Frequently the biblical term, heart, is better than soul.) Such a description is a caricature of the theology of grace, but it does correspond to the primary emphasis in many present day textbooks on grace.

Theologians today stress what they call uncreated grace and not created grace. Grace itself means a free gift—the free gift of God communicating himself to us. God is giving himself to us as our Father. Grace is first and foremost an "I-thou" relationship between the loving and the merciful Father and the helpless and sinful creature. In the Holy Spirit and through Jesus Christ, the only Son of God, we are constituted sons in the Son, sons of the heavenly Father and his family and brothers and sisters of all those who share this new life. Grace is not a thing—it is a relation. Thanks to the great gift of God we together can pray, "Our Father, who art in heaven."

The whole task of the Christian life is the development of my relationship with God and with my brothers and sisters. I will be a perfect child of God only in heaven. Here on earth the Christian must consciously strive to become a more perfect child of the heavenly Father and a more perfect brother of the God-man himself, Jesus Christ.

Likewise, sin is no longer seen as a blot on the soul or even as the breaking of a law. Sin is ultimately the breaking of the relationship with God, the refusal to accept his love, the prodigal son's taking his inheritance and leaving the house of his father. We must pay attention to external acts especially insofar as they manifest and make visible the heart of man. Man in his heart is either, through grace, a friend of God or his enemy. External acts have a meaning only insofar as they manifest this inner reality and confirm or deepen the individual in the state he has chosen. Heretofore we have paid too much attention to particular, external acts as sins and failed to realize there is only one sin—the refusal to accept God as our Father. Sin also disrupts the bond joining all men in the family of God. We must stress more the social and communitarian aspect of sin.

Likewise, a more personalist approach to the sacraments is prevalent today. Previously we have over-emphasized the fact that the sacraments work *ex opere operato*. Some people then tend to think there is no need for personal disposition. Sacramentalism in practice has frequently degenerated almost to a form of magic. Think, for example, of the popular concept of the anointing of the sick. Make sure the patient has the priest before he dies. But barrels of holy oil will not save the person unless he is disposed to accept God as his Father. An almost magical concept of the sacraments underlies the great insistence on quantity and numbers. We fail to see that it must also be a question of quality.

Most people believe that the priest, because he is the celebrant of the Mass, receives a special grace and fruit. I cannot accept such an assertion. Remember, the Mass of itself can add nothing to Calvary. Christ is the perfect priest and perfect victim of the one, perfect sacrifice. The individual Mass exists only to bring the Christian community into contact with the sacrifice of Christ. The fruits and values of the Mass here and now depend *only* on the dispositions of those present; that is, on the extent to which they enter into the sacrifice. My personal dispositions are independent of my priesthood. There are times when I personally am more disposed by participating fully in the Mass (i.e., also receiving Communion) as a member of the Christian community gathered around the banquet table of the Lord.

The sacraments are an encounter or personal meeting between God and man. The sacraments are acts of the risen Christ coming into contact with me here and now. Man must respond to God's advance. The comparison of the sacrament with the matrimonial embrace is most apt. The loving sacramental embrace of Christ should evoke a response on our part. The coldness of our hearts should melt in the warmth of his embrace.

A personalist concept of the sacraments does not destroy the efficacy of the sacraments. The sacraments do produce grace *ex opere operato*. But *ex opere operato* means that the sacrament is an act of God here and now communicating himself to the believer. Man must be disposed to accept God's loving gift of himself. There were many who came into contact with Christ during the period of his earthly life, but only a few were disposed to receive him.

THE BIBLICAL RENEWAL

The greatest influence in the renewal of theology is the return to the scriptures and the Fathers. Biblical and patristic studies have contributed greatly to all the areas of renewal already mentioned. We will concentrate on what appears to be the most important single topic in the current renewal—the resurrection in the work of the redemption and the life of the Christian.

For too long, theology considered the redemption almost exclusively under the categories of merit and satisfaction. God's justice demanded satisfaction for the infinite offense of the sins of man. God's own Son by his death on the cross paid the necessary price for our redemption. Some theological descriptions of the redemption by the death of Christ almost picture God the Father as a sadist!

The resurrection was considered only as an appendage, something that happened after our redemption was already won by the death of Christ. The main consideration of the resurrection heretofore was for apologetic reasons. The resurrection is the greatest miracle wrought by Christ. It proves he was the legate or ambassador of God and spoke the truth.

The biblical perspective puts the resurrection in the heart of the mystery of redemption. For St. Paul, the redemption is a drama having its premiere in Christ himself, and played again in every Christian. Redemption is a sanctifying transformation from death to life, from darkness to light. The Son of God in a free act of love took upon himself flesh and a sinful human nature. Since Adam, flesh and sin have been synonymous with separation from God. Christ accepted such a state, which could lead only to death, but death was not the end. Death was only one point in the whole process of transformation or passing over from death to life. The divine victim was transformed into the newness of the life of the resurrection. The redemption was accomplished.

The exodus in which the Israelites left Egypt and passed over into the promised land, as well as the passover meal that commemorated it, are dim forbearers of the passing over from death to life which took place in the resurrection and its commemoration in the Eucharistic meal. Scripture portrays the resurrection as the work of the Father, who in pouring out his Spirit raised his Son from the dead and made him the Lord, the Son of God in power. In raising his Son, the Father inaugurated the Church. In his resurrection Christ becomes the new Adam, the first born of the new creation, the head of the body of Christ.

The individual Christian is saved insofar as he enters into the mystery of redemption, the transformation from death to life. The baptism of the individual Christian is the continuation of the work of the Father of handing over his Son and raising him from the dead. In baptism we are transformed; we die and rise with Christ in the newness of life. Through the Church and the sacraments of the Church, the members of God's family nourish their new life and strengthen their relationship of love with the heavenly Father and with one another. Suffering, mortification, and sacrifice have a meaning as part of the dying to self and rising to God. The whole Christian life is the living of the Paschal mystery, the passing over from death to life. Salvation is primarily the work of God, an *opus a Deo operatum*.

The mystery of the resurrection sheds light on the Christian attitude toward death. The Christian dies but once, at baptism, when he dies to sin. Physical death is not the end; it is not to be feared. Rather it is a joyful event, a going home to the eternal house of the Father. Death begins the living of the perfect life of the resurrection.

Perhaps it is not an exaggeration to say that the resurrection is at the center of the whole renewal in the Church today. Theology is the study of the Paschal Mystery in Christ and in the life of every Christian. Liturgy is the celebration of the Paschal Mystery. Preaching is the joyful announcing of the Paschal Mystery.

This chapter has sketched three major influences in the present day renewal of theology. Perhaps it will also serve to arouse a greater appreciation of the nature of theology. The student of theology does not approach his subject like the student of mathematics or architecture or literature. He approaches theology in the reverent posture of a worshiper in spirit and truth. Theology is not sterile intellectualism. It does not consist in truths to be memorized. Theology is the study of him who is love and of his rallying call to all creatures to share forever in his love in the family of God.

The Christian
Conscience Today

Chapter Two

Even a superficial reflection shows the existence of moral conscience. Man experiences the joy of having done good or the remorse of having done evil. He recognizes an imperative to do this or avoid that. A more profound analysis distinguishes moral conscience from social pressure or even a religious imperative.[1]

Moral conscience has many meanings. St. Paul describes conscience as a witness or judge of past activity, a director of future action, the habitual quality of a man's Christianity, and even as the Christian ego or personality.[2] This chapter will discuss the problem of antecedent conscience; that is, conscience as pointing out to the Christian what he should do in the particular circumstances of his life.

Scripture reveals Christianity as a dialogue or covenant relationship between God and his people. Christian tradition frequently refers to conscience as the voice of God telling man how to respond to the divine gift of salvation. Both the reality and the concept of moral conscience have evolved in the course of salvation history. Two reasons explain the evolution. First, God speaks to primitive man in one way and to more mature man in another way. Second, only when man has acquired a certain degree of maturity can he reflect on his own subjective states.[3]

In the beginning of salvation history, conscience (the reality, not the word) appears as extrinsic, objective, and collective.[4] Theophany, however, gives way to angelophany, and finally to human prophets who speak in the name of God.[5] The prophets, the conscience of Israel, stress interior dispositions and begin to mention individual responsibility (Jer 31:29-30; Ez 14:1-8). They look forward to the day when God will plant his law in the innermost part of man (Jer 31:33-34; Ez 36:26-27; Psalm 50:12). Since the prophets insist on God as the first cause, conscience is not the voice of man but the voice of God who speaks to man.

St. Paul, with his emphasis on the internal and subjective dispositions of man, brings into Christian thought the term conscience (συνείδησις), which originally appeared in Democritus and was developed by stoic philosophy.[6] Paul, while adopting the uses of the term in pagan philosophy, introduces the notion of conscience as the director of human activity—antecedent conscience.[7] Commenting on the different Pauline uses of the term conscience, the Fathers of the church explicitly make the last step in the interiorization of conscience. Conscience now becomes the voice of the human person himself and only mediately and indirectly the voice of God.[8]

Scholastic theology of the thirteenth century first considered scientifically, as opposed to the pastoral approach of the Fathers, the nature of moral conscience. Is it a faculty? A habit? An act? The Thomistic school distinguished conscience, the judgment of the practical reason about a particular act, from synteresis, the quasi-innate habit of the first principles of the moral order. St. Bonaventure placed more emphasis on the will, especially with regard to synteresis. The subjective voice of reason was open to God through the mediation of law.[9]

Unfortunately, the scholastic synthesis succumbed to the dangers of sterile intellectualism, the nominalistic tendency to extrinsicism, and the increasing influence of positive juridic sciences. The decree of the Council of Trent again legislating the necessity of annual confession of sins according to their number and species orientated moral theology (and the question of conscience) toward the judgment seat of the confessional rather than toward the living of the Christian life.[10]

In this light one can better understand the famous controversy of the seventeenth and eighteenth centuries about the question of a probable conscience. When I am not certain about the existence of a law, am I obliged to follow the doubtful law? Today the vast majority of moral theologians accept some form of a mitigated probabilism, which maintains that only a law which is certain can oblige a subject.[11] As a result of the controversy, *De Conscientia* became a separate and well-developed treatise in the manuals of moral theology. Among the benefits accruing to moral theology from such a development are the balance and equilibrium finally attained, the precise terminology acquired, and the realization that conscience must consider the many problems of daily living.

However, the defects of the manualistic treatises on conscience are great. Briefly, legalism, extrinicism, impersonalism, and an ethic of obligation characterize such considerations of conscience. Positive law and objective considerations are greatly exaggerated. Conscience becomes negative, oppressive, and sin-orientated.[12] The dire consequences are not restricted merely to the intellectual and theoretical plane. History and empirical studies show that the linking of introspection with a legalistic approach to morality provides fertile ground for the formation of the scrupulous conscience.[13] Unfortunately, in everyday Catholic life, the average Catholic equates Christian morality with Mass on Sunday, no meat on Friday, and the need to obey what the Church teaches about sex.

In the last few decades theologians have begun to react against the manualistic treatment of conscience. Under the influence of the Thomistic renewal, authors now stress the virtue of prudence and the subjective element which cannot be found in any of the books on cases of conscience.[14] In keeping with the return to the primitive sources of scripture and the Fathers, which is characterizing all theological investigation today, theologians consider conscience in the light of charity, or the responsibility of the Christian before the call of God, or as an anticipation of the eschatological judgment.[15]

Outside the pale of theology, two divergent tendencies—exaggerated interiorization and over-objectivization—have destroyed the true notion of conscience. Ever since Descartes, philosophers like Montaigne, Rousseau, and Kant have overemphasized the subjective element. Existentialism, the last step in the tendency, makes subjective conscience the center of the whole world completely cut off from God or any other subject. At the other extreme, conscience is considered merely a function of physiological factors (Chauchard), psychological factors (Freud), or sociological factors (Durkheim).[16]

THE NATURE OF CONSCIENCE

Guided by the lessons of history, one can better understand the nature of conscience, its function, and its formation. Catholic theologians generally distinguish synteresis, moral science, and conscience. Adopting a synthetic approach, we can define synteresis as the power of conscience situated in the inmost part of the soul (*scintilla animae*). In its rational aspect, synteresis tends to the truth so that man almost intuitively knows the fundamental principle of the moral order—good is to be done and evil is to be avoided. In its volitional aspect, synteresis tends toward the good and the expression of such a tendency in action.

Moral science is the knowledge of the less general principles of the moral law which man deduces from the primary principles. The category of moral knowledge also includes whatever man knows from revelation or authority. It pertains to the objective, the conceptual, the essential order.

Conscience is the concrete judgment of the practical reason, made under the twofold influence of synteresis, about the moral goodness of a particular act. Conscience forms its judgment discursively from the objective principles of the moral order; but at the same time, there is also a direct connatural knowing process. The dictate of conscience is concrete, subjective, individual, and existential.

Conscience tells man what he should do. Man's "ought" follows from his "is." Man's actions must affirm his being. St. Paul makes Christian existence the foundation of Christian morality. The Christian is baptized into the death and resurrection of Christ. Consequently, he must die to self and walk in the newness of life (Rom 6). Man's existence is a loving dependence on his God and a communion with his fellow men. Human endeavor must express this twofold personal relationship.

Conscience and human freedom are not completely autonomous. In practice man rejects the complete autonomy of conscience. In the eyes of the world Adolf Eichmann and the Nazis were guilty of crimes against humanity despite the plea of a clear conscience. Conscience must act in accord with the nature and person of man. The greatest possible freedom and the greatest possible happiness for man consist in the fulfillment of his own being.

The judgment of conscience expresses with regard to a particular act the fundamental tendency of man to truth and good. The basis of Christian morality, however, is not man's relation to an abstract principle, but to a person, *the* person, God. Since he first loved us, God has freely given us his love, his friendship, our salvation. Scripture uses the words faith and love (πίστις, ἀγάπη) to express man's acceptance and response to God's gift. Like Christ himself, man's external actions must manifest this love. At the same time man's actions dispose him to enter more intimately into the mystery of divine love. The ultimate norm of Christian conduct is this: what does the love of God demand of me in these concrete circumstances? Love, as a complete giving of self and not a mere emotion, seeks always the will of the beloved.

THE FORMATION OF CONSCIENCE

God speaks to us through the very existence he has given us—creation, salvation, our talents, abilities and even weaknesses, and the existential circumstances of our situation. In other words, the will of the beloved is made known to us through his "laws"—the law of the Spirit, the natural law. positive law, and the law of the situation.[17]

The primary law of the new covenant is the internal law of the Spirit, the law of Christ, the law of love. Even Christ, however, found it necessary to express his law in external rules; but the demands are comparatively general; e.g., the beatitudes.[18]

God also speaks to man through the human nature he has given him. The natural law, as theologians call it, is primarily a dynamic, internal law. Since it is the very law of man's existence and being, it has an absolute character.[19] Christ, at least implicitly, affirmed the value of the natural law within the framework of the new covenant.[20] The law of nature is assumed into the law of Christ, for all nature was created according to the image of Christ and all nature exists for Christ.[21] From the first principle of the natural law, more objective, detailed rules of conduct are formulated.

Unfortunately, many Catholic theologians have exaggerated the natural law. It is not the primary law for the Christian. Some have succumbed to the temptation of using the natural law as a club. Others have overextended it in attempting to prove the moral certitude of mere hypotheses. Many still tend to codify completely the natural law and thus rob the natural law of its dynamic character.

Living in human society, the Christian is also the subject of human law, both civil and ecclesiastical. Such law is purely external and consequently seen as an infringement on human liberty. Since positive legislation is not absolute, it does not oblige when in conflict with the interest of the higher laws.

God has called each person by his own name. In one sense, every individual is unique; every concrete situation is unique. The Christian's answer to the divine call must correspond to his individual circumstances.

Conscience is a supernaturally elevated subjective power of man. The law of Christ and the natural law are primarily internal laws. Why then is it necessary to have detailed, particular, external expressions of these laws? Why a code? Man's love of God is not yet perfect. Fallen human nature still experiences the tendency to self and not to God. Spiritual schizophrenia is a necessary characteristic of earthly Christianity. Even the impulsive reaction of the human will of Christ was to avoid the sacrifice willed by his father.[22] Love of God is by its nature a self-sacrificing love. Man in his present state cannot know perfectly what the demands of love of God are. Particular, external expressions of the law of love and natural law have a value only insofar as they point out the minimum and basic demands of the law of love. Code morality is not opposed to an ethic of love.[23]

External law, if considered without any relation to the internal law, can be even an occasion of sin (Gal 3:19, Rom 5:20-21; 7:5-23). The external law is static and very incomplete. It does not and cannot express the totality of man's relationship to God. The vast majority of the decisions of conscience pertains to matters where there are no determined external expressions of law. Thus far we have not been speaking of the positive human laws which are primarily external. Here, too, self-sacrificing love of God and respect for the common good move man to obey positive law despite its inherent imperfections, unless such positive law runs counter to a higher law.

The formation and training of conscience include much more than the mere knowledge of external formulas of law. Insistence on external law is the haven of the insecure (neuroticism, scrupulosity) or the shallow (legalism, Phariseeism). Christian morality is ultimately love, an "I-thou" relationship between God and man. By meditating on true values, the Christian grows in wisdom and age and grace. Likewise, the formation of conscience must take into consideration the findings of many of the positive sciences. For example, what purports to be religious obedience might in reality be the manifestation of an inferiority complex. A proper formation, joined with the virtue of prudence acquired in daily Christian experiences, prepares the conscience to hear the call of God's love.

Space permits the mention of only two important characteristics of Christian conscience: communitarian and creative. A communitarian conscience recognizes man's relationship with his fellow men in the kingdom of God. A communitarian conscience avoids excessive individualism and the opposite extreme of mass hypnosis. A creative conscience, attuned to the Spirit, throws off the shackles of stultifying legalism. A true Christian conscience leads man to make Christianity and Christian love "the light of the world and the salt of the earth"—a positive commitment to the kingdom of God in its reality both as the city of God and the city of man.

Reality is complex. The problems of conscience are complex. Frequently, there are no easy solutions. After prayerful consideration of all values involved, the Christian chooses what he believes to be the demands of love in the present situation. The Christian can never expect to have perfect, mathematical certitude about his actions. The virtue of humility preserves him from falling into the opposed extremes of introspective anxiety and mere formalism. Neurotic anxiety has no place in Christianity. Christianity is fundamentally a religion of joy—of man's participation in the joy and triumph of the resurrection. The paradox of Christianity is that joy comes through self-sacrificing love.

For the Christian who has made a commensurate effort to form his conscience correctly, the dictate of conscience is an infallible norm of conduct. Even though the action itself is not in objective conformity with the divine will, the Christian's conduct is pleasing to God, for it stems from a pure heart.[24]

The opposition that conscience experiences between Christian law and Christian freedom, between love and code morality, stems from man's imperfect love of God and wounded human nature. In reality, there is no dichotomy. The Christian law is the law of love—"the law of the Spirit, [giving] life in Christ Jesus, has delivered me from the law of sin and death" (Rom 8:2). Conscience leads man to participate ever more deeply in Christian love and freedom until the Christian reaches his final destiny where love, joy, freedom, and conformity with God's will are one.

Notes for Chapter 2

1.
Jacques Leclercq, *Les grandes lignes de la philosophie morale* (Louvain, 1953), pp. 7-13.

2.
C. Spicq, "La conscience dans le Nouveau Testament," *Revue Biblique* 47 (1938), pp. 55-76. Cf., C. A. Pierce, *Conscience in the New Testament* (London, 1955).

3.
For the general lines of the evolution by which God brought his people in the Old Testament to both self-knowledge and a knowledge of the true God, see Marc Oraison, *Love or Constraint?* (New York, 1959), pp. 152-163.

4.
The characteristics of a primitive conscience in general are aptly described by Richard Mohr, *Die Christliche Ethik im Lichte der Ethnologie* (München, 1954).

5.
Theophany abounds in the first chapters of Genesis. There is some dispute among scripture scholars on the exact nature of the "Angel of Yahweh" which appears in Genesis 16:7; 22:11; Exodus 3:2; Judges 2:1. Even if the expression here refers merely to God in a visible form, such an expression indicates a "sophisticated" reluctance to speak of a pure theophany. In the Old Testament, angels exercise the same twofold function as conscience; namely, they make known the will of God and serve as guides both for individuals and the whole people of God.

6.
Spicq, pp. 51-55; Pierce, pp. 13-53. Also Th. Deman, *La Prudence* (Paris, 1949), pp. 479-487.

7.
Eric D'Arcy, *Conscience and its Right to Freedom* (New York, 1961), pp. 8-12; Pietro Palazzini, *La Coscienza* (Rome, 1961), pp. 63-71; Deman, pp. 488-489. Spicq maintains that the concept of an antecedent conscience was known by Paul's contemporaries, but it is certain that Paul contributed the most to its development (pp. 63-67). Among the texts cited as instances of Paul's referring to antecedent conscience are: 1 Cor 8; 10:25-33; Rom 13:5.

8.
The affirmation is made by Antonio Hortelano in unpublished notes. Hortelano refers to the following citations from *Cursus Completus Patrologiae*, ed. J. P. Migne (Paris). Augustinus, "Tractatus in Joannem," *Pat. Latina* 35, col. 1382; Origines, "Commentarium in Epistolam ad Romanos," *Pat. Graeca* 14, col. 895; Basilius, "Homilia XIII," *Pat. Graeca* 31, col. 432.

9.
Odon Lottin, *Morale Fondamentale* (Tournai, 1954), pp. 163-165; 221-228. The author summarizes here the conclusions derived from his multi-volumed historical study, *Psychologie et Morale aux XII*e *et XIII*e *siècles* (Gembloux).

10.
There is no complete and authentic history of moral theology. Nor can there be until more particular studies are made. For the best available study of the development of moral theology of this time, see Bernard Häring—Louis Vereecke, "La Théologie Morale de S. Thomas d'Aquin à S. Alphonse de Liguori," *Nouvelle Revue Théologique* 77 (1955), pp. 673-692. Also Louis Vereecke, "Le Council de Trente et l'enseignement de la Théologie Morale," *Divinitas* 5 (1961), pp. 361-374.

11.
Most of the manuals of moral theology accept such a probabilism. In practice, the antiprobabilists do not differ much from those who espouse simple probabilism. Outside the manuals, there is a reaction against the legalistic mentality of probabilism which has taken different forms. Cf., Th. Deman, "Probabilisme," *Dictionnaire de Théologie Catholique* 13 (Paris, 1936), col. 417-619; also Deman, *La Prudence;* Georges Leclercq, *La Conscience du Chrétien* (Paris, 1947), pp. 127-197; P. Rousselot, *Quaestiones de Conscientia* (Paris, 1947), pp. 51-80.

12.
The increasing awareness of the need for a renewal of moral theology in the last few years stems from these negative characteristics present today in most manuals. For a brief review of the recent literature on the subject of renewing moral theology, see John C. Ford and Gerald Kelly, *Contemporary Moral Theology* (Westminster, Md., 1958), pp. 42-103. It is my personal belief that the authors have not paid sufficient attention to the part played by the Tübingen school of theology, nor do they seem to fully appreciate the need for a life-centered and not confessional-orientated moral theology.

13.
Juan Garcia-Vicente, "Dirección pastoral de la escrupulosidad," *Revista de Espiritualidad* 19 (1960), pp. 514-529. Also,

Cahiers Laënnec 20 (June 1960) which is totally concerned with the question of scrupulosity.

14.
Deman, *La Prudence*, especially pp. 496-514. Perhaps Deman overemphasizes prudence at the expense of conscience. For a very satisfying discussion of the relationship between prudence and conscience, see Domenico Capone, *Intorno alla verità morale* (Naples, 1951). A fuller bibliography on the relationship between prudence and conscience is given by Josephus Fuchs, *Theologia Moralis Generalis* (Rome, 1960), p. 169.

15.
Bernard Häring, *The Law of Christ I* (Westminster, Md., 1961), pp. 91-213; René Carpentier, "Conscience," *Dictionnaire de Spiritualité* 2 (Paris, 1953), col. 1548-1575; Gérard Gilleman, "Eros ou agapè, Comment centrer la conscience chrétienne," *Nouvelle Revue Théologique* 72 (1950), pp. 3-26; 113-135.

16.
For a critique of such opinions based on theological principles, see Palazzini, pp. 217-275. Also, Jacques Leclercq, *Christ and the Modern Conscience* (New York, 1962), pp. 7-104.

17.
The word law is not a univocal term. Unfortunately, the coercive characteristic which essentially belongs to external positive law has been illegitimately transferred to the law of the Spirit and the natural law.

18.
Some of Christ's laws are materially determined and particular; e.g., with regard to divorce, adultery, or even the thought of adultery. For an explanation of the general and more formal demands of Christ as the expression of a mentality or tendency rather than a determined material command, see C. H. Dodd, *Gospel and Law* (Cambridge, 1951), pp. 73-83.

19.
A good description of the natural law with regard to its internal and historical character as well as its relationship to the law of Christ is given by J. Fuchs, *Le Droit Naturel: Essai Théologique* (Tournai, 1960).

20.
Matt 5:27-48; 19:3-12, 17-20; Mark 7:20-23; Luke 12:57.

21.
For Christ as the exemplar of all creation and nature, see Col 1:15-20; 1 Cor 8:6; Eph 1:3-10. Theologians speak of Christ as the final cause of all creation because of the same texts as well as John 1:1-14 and 1 Cor 3:22-23.

22.
Matt 26:39. Theologians, interpreting the different acts of the will of Christ in this passage, distinguish between the *voluntas ut natura* and the *voluntas ut ratio*. Christ's human will impulsively shrank from suffering. He could accept suffering only insofar as he saw it as the will of his Father.

23.
For the Catholic, the magisterium or teaching function of the Church gives an authentic interpretation of Christian morality. Doctrinal and moral pronouncements constitute just one aspect of the teaching office of the Church. The whole Church in the lives of all members must bear living witness to the truth.

24.
During the probabilism controversy, anti-probabilists frequently cited the opinion of St. Bernard that a person following an erroneous conscience in good faith commits sin. Bernard's opinion stems from his mystical insistence on conscience as the voice of God. Consequently, any error or deviation can be attributed only to the bad will of man. Philippe Delhaye, *Le problème de la conscience morale chez S. Bernard* (Namur, 1957), especially pp. 44-45.

Formation in Freedom
and Responsibility

Chapter Three

Why the interest today in freedom and responsibility? Is it just a fad like the Beatles and the frug and spring vacations at Lauderdale? Perhaps the question of freedom and responsibility is not just a fad but rather a symptom of youth—a stage that everyone must pass through in his growth and development. No. The problem of authority and obedience, responsibility and freedom is a very deep reality today. Why?

Philosophically, modern thinkers of all schools are placing more emphasis on the dignity of the human person with his inviolable rights and freedoms. An obligation-oriented ethic stemming from Kant has given way to a modern personalism. The present teaching in the Church on religious liberty owes its development to a greater appreciation of the dignity and value of the human person.

Modern political thought also emphasizes the freedom and responsibility of the individual person. People are citizens and no longer subjects whose lives are completely governed by those in authority. Whereas totalitarianism constitutes the greatest enemy of individual freedom and responsibility, the principle of subsidiarity tries to safeguard individual rights and values. Conscientious Christians are appalled at the lack of individual responsibility before the injustices perpetrated by modern governments. Where were the responsible people to speak out against the excesses of authority committed in world society in the last few decades? Here we must be careful not to see just one side of the coin; e.g., what happened in Nazi Germany. How many of us Americans spoke out against the immoral bombing of cities and population centers?

Likewise, the sociological structure of modern society is no longer based on a concept of blind obedience. Democracies are springing up in political life; the patriarchal society no longer structures family life; complex modern economic and business life demands initiative and creativity that cannot be found in authoritarian structures.[1]

Philosophically, politically, and sociologically, modern man is rethinking the concepts of freedom and responsibility, authority and obedience. Naturally the question arises about freedom and responsibility for the Christian. The Vatican Council has proposed a twofold principle for all renewal in the Church—a greater understanding of the revealed truths of Christianity and a true adaptation to the needs of the modern world. In the age of the Vatican Council we must apply the same principles of renewal to the question of freedom and responsibility. The sincere questioner must admit that for many years the prevailing understanding of freedom and responsibility in the Church expressed neither the biblical ideas nor the needs of modern man but rather mirrored concepts that belonged to a particular period of secular history.

The present discussion then is theological—the theological basis for a spiritual formation in freedom and responsibility. What is freedom? There are numerous understandings of freedom. All agree that freedom does not mean indulgence. Otherwise, freedom and responsibility could not be correlative terms. Nor is freedom primarily a question of free choice or free will as the manuals of theology and philosophy generally consider it. Man soon realizes that every external choice limits his external freedom with regard to other objects. Freedom is primarily internal and not external, although the external freedom must exist as the manifestation of true internal freedom.

The true freedom of the children of God is the gift of the Holy Spirit, the *donum Spiritus Sancti*, to which Christians must open themselves. Freedom is the spontaneous creativity of the human person to realize himself. Man realizes himself as a creature of God redeemed not by his own merits but by his rebirth through water and the Spirit. The Spirit imparts to man the new life of the children of God. "And where the Spirit of the Lord is, there is freedom" (2 Cor 3:17). Through the life-giving Spirit we receive our adoption as sons. Since the love of God is in us, we can cry out, "Abba Father." We are sons and not slaves. The Spirit is the principle and giver of our new life and our freedom. Hence the Christian life is a vocation to love and to freedom. The Christian paradox is that freedom consists in the total abandonment of self to the Spirit. The demands of the Spirit are total and ruthless, but only the Spirit who gives life and freedom can fulfill the cravings of restless mankind.

A truly spiritual theology is the unifying theme behind all the considerations of freedom and responsibility. The freedom that the Spirit gives entails the responsibility of opening oneself to the demands of the Spirit. Selfishness and indulgence are the direct opposite of the life of the Spirit. Christ has freed us from sin which is basically selfishness and egoism. Christians who have received the new life of the Spirit must walk in the light and not in the darkness. This chapter will treat various theological problems connected with the question of freedom and responsibility, but all these divergent considerations bring into sharper focus the primary place of the Spirit in the Christian life.

THE SPIRIT AND THE LAW

The Christian life is primarily a life of love—the love of God is poured out in our hearts by the Holy Spirit who is given to us. The Spirit makes us the loving children of the Father, sons in the Son, and directs all our activity from within. If with Saint Paul we do speak of the law of the Spirit (Rom 8:2), it is not a law in a sense of a coercive force that is oppressing us from outside. For the Christian who is under the Spirit there is no coercion; his actions are prompted by the love of God.

Christians then must be educated in their vocation to love and in their vocation to freedom. External laws are not the be-all and the end-all of Christianity. Their limited purpose is to bring Christians to love; their role is secondary and relative in the new dispensation. Christianity is primarily a religion of love and freedom, and all its externals must be sacramental signs of its inner reality. Unfortunately in practice and in the mentality of people external law frequently has usurped the primary place. Some in the Church today are discussing the abolition of the Lenten fast and the Friday abstinence. Many people object that the Church is becoming too soft and giving in to a spirit of easy living. Such an objection implies that without a law there will be no sacrifice. For those who put all their trust in the law and its coercion, Christianity itself is meaningless. Worse yet, God is dead. This is the atheism of legalism. If Christians cannot use properly Christian means in the motivating of people, then is it any wonder that Christianity frequently becomes irrelevant and says nothing to the modern world? Those who rely primarily on law and its sanctions can be more unchristian than those they condemn.

Christians today need more faith in Christ and in the way that he chose. He could have forced all men into his kingdom, but rather he wanted man to freely respond to the call of his love. So often present day practice seems to think that God has made a mistake, that he has put too much trust in man, that God was too optimistic. People will only understand force and its application. But who are we to question the wisdom of God? Rather we must conform our ways to his. The Paschal Mystery gives testimony to the extent of God's love in giving and protecting the freedom of his creatures.

Many voices today rightly condemn legalism; but there exists an even more deeply ingrained error—pelagianism. Pelagianism is the heresy of self-sufficiency. The Paschal Mystery reminds us that as Christ was raised from the dead, so we too have been raised into the newness of life. The perennial temptation, from Adam to the present day, is to play God. Man wants to know all things, to have all the answers, to control all things, to legislate all things. If only man could tie everything into neat little bundles with no loose ends! What we need is some confusion to remind us that we are the poor of Yahweh who depend completely on him for our salvation.

A subtle pelagianism leads to mediocrity. The spirit calls man to a constant and complete giving of himself. As an earthly pilgrim, the Christian can never put down his bags and rest content. External norms, by providing a standard that man can rather easily attain, furnish a crutch which provides a false sense of security. A regime of external law is not as demanding as the life of the Spirit. The timid and weak man hides in the shadow of the law lest he be forced to accept the responsibilities of the freedom of the sons of God.

For Christians in the world, pilgrim Christians who are not yet completely under the Spirit, some external laws will always be necessary. The external law must point out the minimal demands of love to those whose sin and flesh might still attract them to selfishness and sin and not to love. But the role of external law in the Christian economy is secondary and relative. External law is not the directing principle of all Christian action, but only the indication of some minimal Christian obligations.

Yes, there is a danger in putting the emphasis on the Spirit and not on the law. Some Christians will always abuse the freedom of the children of God, but abuse should not take away the use *(abusus non tollit usum)*. St. Paul recognized the danger of abuse and reminded Christians that precisely through the Spirit they had died to the slavery of sin and selfishness. Consider especially the attitude of Christ. No one knew better than Christ the terrible abuse of freedom, but he came into the world to give us our freedom. Perhaps present day Christians do not put enough trust in Christ.

THE THOMISTIC CONCEPT OF MAN

The cornerstone of Thomistic moral theology, according to the Prologue to the Second Part of the *Summa Theologiae*, is man, insofar as he is an image of God. After considering God in the first part of the *Summa*, Thomas then considers man, his image, according as he is "endowed with intelligence, free will, and a power of actions which is proper to him . . . having a dominion over his own activity." Man participates in and assimilates more and more the divine perfection insofar as he is *"sui potestativus."*[2] Thomas develops his moral thought without reference to the concepts of obligation and law itself which come near the end of Thomas' consideration of human moral activity. Thomas is not the last word or the only word in Catholic thought, but Thomas was an adversary of all legalism and obligationalism in moral thinking.

How often have we educators failed to put into practice the basic Thomistic insight that man is an image of God according as he freely directs his own activity! Frequently we submit to the temptation of becoming administrators and not educators. At times it appears much easier to make laws than to educate for the true and the good; but the mechanical, routine observance of laws is not true Christian moral activity according to St. Thomas. Thomas' concept of man's moral activity demands a great responsibility, the responsibility of determining one's actions according to the true and the good.

HUMAN LAW

Catholic theology embraces two divergent traditions on the understanding of human laws. While most manuals of theology, canon law, and philosophy cite the Thomistic definition of law, their interpretation and understanding of law is Scotistic or Suarezian rather than Thomistic. The Thomistic concept emphasizes law as an act of reason ordering to the common good, whereas the Scotistic school (developed by Suarez) places primary emphasis on the will act of the legislator. For Thomas something is commanded because it is good. For the voluntarists something is good because it is commanded. Nominalistic philosophy has greatly influenced the voluntaristic notion of law. According to Thomas the obligation of law stems from the connection of the act with the common good and not from the will of the legislator. A Thomistic concept of law and its obligation rests on the intrinsic connection between the act commanded and the common good and not merely on the extrinsic will of the legislator. The will of the legislator is not supreme; but rather the task of ordering to the common good is the primary function of the human legislator.[3]

A consideration of human law naturally brings up the connection between law and sin. Good theology avoids the mistake of saying that certain laws oblige under pain of mortal sin.[4] Mortal sin is not primarily a penalty or a punishment, but rather the reality of man's breaking his relationship with God. But it is also misleading to speak of the binding force of laws in terms of mortal sin. Mortal sin ultimately involves the fundamental choice of man's existence, his project of existence. Even the often repeated threefold conditions for mortal sin (at best, these are just presumptive norms to follow) remind us of the difference between law and sin. It would be better for the Church to propose its laws in terms of the greater or lesser importance of a particular action but without mentioning the existence of sin. (However, the Church must honestly ask how important are such things as Friday abstinence, Lenten fast, and praying the breviary.) Thus, human law would not assume primary importance in Christian morality.

EPIKEIA

The different concepts of law determine different notions of epikeia. Most textbooks teach the Suarezian concept of epikeia. Epikeia is usually considered very dangerous because man uses it to sneak out from the obligations of law. Generally textbooks restrict epikeia to the cases where the circumstances unforeseen by the legislator would indicate that it was not his mind or intention to bind the subject in a particular case. The general tenor of the teaching is that epikeia may not be used if recourse to the legislator is possible. The determining element is the will of the legislator who would not want to bind his subject under these particular circumstances.

St. Thomas, on the other hand, begins his treatment by showing that epikeia is a virtue.[5] Epikeia is a part of the virtue of legal justice; in fact, epikeia is the *"quasi superior regula humanorum actuum."*[6] Justice demands the existence of epikeia because of the inherent imperfection of human law.

In particular there are many reasons for the existence of the virtue of epikeia. First, the relationship of the individual person to the community or society is not a relationship of complete subordination. There will always be a tension between the legitimate needs of the individual and the community. Epikeia prevents the total submission of the individual to the demands of the common good. Thus, for example, personal impossibility might excuse one from a particular duty for the common good. Secondly, the primary law of Christianity is the internal law of the Spirit. All external law is relative to the demands of the higher law of the Spirit. There can be occasions when the higher law demands that we not observe the letter of the external law. Thirdly, human law by its very nature is imperfect; it obliges *ut in pluribus.* Positive law is not based on the unchangeable essences but on the changing circumstances. The more people covered by the law and the greater the variety of circumstances in which they live, the greater will be the number of exceptions to the law. The rapidly changing sociological conditions of modern life only accent the need in justice for the virtue of epikeia. Fourthly, human error can exist on the part of the lawgiver. Most Americans are willing to admit that prohibition was a mistake; likewise many ecclesiastics admit that *Veterum Sapientia* was an unjust law.

Epikeia then is the lubricating oil which allows for a smooth relationship between the essentially relative and imperfect human laws and the higher laws of Christianity—the law of the Spirit and the natural law. Epikeia is not lawlessness—the sneaking out from the obligations of a positive law. Rather, epikeia is the response to the demands of a higher law in a particular situation. Others object that epikeia is the worst kind of subjectivism and leads to anarchy because it makes the individual the final judge of whether he will observe the law or not.

The answer to the above charge of anarchy is an emphatic "no." Remember that epikeia is a demand of the virtue of justice. Epikeia is also the demand of the higher law of the Spirit. The danger of abuse constantly threatens, but the higher law demands that the individual's ultimate motive is not selfishness or egoism. The law of the Spirit has freed us from sin and selfishness. Responsibility rests with the individual to make sure that he is not deceiving himself. Likewise, epikeia supposes the practical judgment of prudence. Prudence is one of the forgotten virtues in our concept of Christian activity, but it must be present in every act. The virtue of epikeia thus becomes an excellent illustration of Christian freedom and responsibility.[7]

The observance of human law for the Christian is a concrete expression of Christian love. Christian love impels the individual to make proportionate sacrifices for the good of the community. Inferiors should even view the inherent imperfections of human law as an opportunity for living the Paschal Mystery—the dying to self and the rising in the newness of life. But, there are times when a higher law supercedes the letter of positive law. The true understanding of epikeia shows the relative character of human law and places responsibility on the individual Christian to be attuned to the demands of the Spirit.

AUTHORITY IN THE CHURCH

The conciliar constitution on the Church marks an end of the juridical and primarily hierarchial concept of the Church which has prevailed for centuries. Now ecclesiology is primarily soteriological and anthropological. The Church is the people of God, the community of the faithful joined with Christ the head and with one another in the bonds of love. Since the Church is an itinerant Church there is still the need for external things—sacraments, authority, churches, etc.; but these structures are temporary and relative, for when the community reaches its eschatological perfection, God's love will be all in all.

Christ, who makes all things new, also renews the concept of authority in the Church. Authority is not domination or the will to power, prestige, and glory. All the people of God must work together for the community. Authority is a loving service which organizes and directs the service and the activities of all for the good of the Church. "The Son of Man also has not come to be served but to serve and to give his life as a ransom for many" (Mark 10:45). Yes, authority in the Church is a power, but Christ compares the greatest in the Church to a child and a servant (Mark 9:32-36). The power base of authority in the Church is love and not coercion. Authority above all demands a leadership in loving service of the people of God.

The temporal and relative character of authority in the Church recalls again the primacy of the Spirit, the source of all life and love in the Church. Authority in the Church speaks for the Spirit, or better, it mediates the Spirit; and consequently must adapt itself to the loving inspirations of the Spirit and not to the domination and trappings of secular authority. Authority in the Church remains always the humble servant of the community and especially of the Spirit.[8]

Frequently, spiritual conferences remind us that the will of the superior is the will of God. Yes, the superior does take the place of God, but not by his act of the will but by his function of ordering for the common good.[9] The superior's authority is not one of domination by imposing his will, but rather of serving the community by organizing the actions of all the members for the good of the community. Hence the need for open dialogue between superiors and inferiors in all levels of the Church. Authority is always necessary, but authority must be ever more conscious of its primary duty to serve the community by ordering for the common good. Authority must ask for and listen to the advice of inferiors. Responsible subjects have an obligation to inform and enlighten their superiors. Also on all levels of authority in the Church the principle of subsidiarity must be exercised. Thus, scripture, theology, and philosophy combine to show authority as a loving service of the community and of the Spirit.

OBEDIENCE

Obedience is not the primary Christian virtue, but obedience is a part of the Christian life. "Blind obedience," however, is foreign to the whole concept of life and authority in the Church. Obedience must be reasonable. St. Thomas defines commanding as the moving of another through the intellect and the will.[10] Blind obedience merits the condemnation of situation ethics, for such obedience pays no attention to what is done but merely considers the motive. There are times when the individual cannot carry out those commands which are not in conformity with the dictates of reason.

The true Christian subject realizes that obedience is a mediation of charity—the sacrifice of oneself for the good of the community. The imperfections of authority offer an opportunity to practice the fullness of dying to self. Since authority occupies a position of viewing the total picture and not just a limited aspect, the presumption always favors the reasonableness of the command. But it can happen that the command is inappropriate or unjust.[11]

THE PROPHETIC OFFICE IN THE CHURCH

Vatican II reminds us that the Church is the people of God. The Holy Spirit dwells in the Church and in the hearts of all the members (*Constitution on the Church*, ¶ 4). "The people of God share also in Christ's prophetic office. . . . It is not only through the sacraments and the ministries of the Church that the Holy Spirit sanctifies and leads the people of God and enriches it with virtues, but, 'allotting his gifts to everyone according as he wills' (1 Cor 12:11), he distributes special graces among the faithful of every rank" (¶ 12).

Today we are quite aware of the prophetic and charismatic element in the Church. Vatican II is proof enough of the renewing power of the Spirit. Thank God for Pope John and the Vatican Council, but it would be a tragic mistake to ascribe the renewal in the Church merely to the Pope and the Council. There would have been no Council if it had not been for the prophets of the biblical, liturgical, catechetical, and ecumenical movements in the Church. History confirms that renewal in the Church is frequently the result of the renewing power of the Spirit in certain of the faithful. History, both ancient and modern, also testifies how the prophets have always suffered for their charism. Just as in the old covenant the *ruah Yahweh* gave the prophets the twofold gift of knowledge and the courage to communicate their message despite their weakness and unwillingness, so too today the prophet needs the inspiration and the courage to announce his message in the face of opposition from the established order. The voice of the Spirit is not limited to the hierarchy and those in authority. All people in the Church, including the hierarchy, must be attentive to the voice of the Spirit in the prophet. The prophet has the tremendous responsibility of being faithful to the inspiration of the Spirit and not using the Spirit for his own selfish aggrandizement.[12] The voice of the prophet is jarring and disconcerting at times, but we must listen. For instance, it could be that John Rock is a modern Isaia.

But there is no dichotomy between the hierarchical Church and the charismatic Church. Authority itself, like all the other charisms, is a gift of the Holy Spirit and is to be exercised under the inspiration of the Spirit for the good of the Church. The Holy Spirit guides authority in making its decisions. Responsible authority in the Church judges and discerns the existence and presence of the Spirit (*Constitution on the Church*, ¶ 13). However, the only absolute authority in the Church is the Holy Spirit. All other authority in the Church is relative and essentially dependent on the Spirit. Except in very few cases authority does not have from the Spirit a guarantee of infallibility. Authorities, like all others in the Church, should humbly listen to the voice of the Spirit. No one person or group of persons has a monopoly on the Holy Spirit; all must listen for the voice of the Spirit speaking in others. Under the Spirit the hierarchy with its divinely appointed mission and all the faithful work together for building up the body of Christ. The pilgrim Church, however, will always know the tension of trying "to practice the truth in love, and so grow up in all things in him who is the head, Christ" (Eph 4:15).[13]

In summary, a formation in freedom and responsibility requires above all a spiritual formation. Timid men shrink from the responsibility of answering the inexorable and ruthless demands of the Spirit. Frequently it appears easier to seek refuge in the seeming security of human law and authority. The Spirit is the source of all life as well as the teacher and the "authority" par excellence in the Church. The Spirit calls for *agape*, the total giving of the Christian, the fullness of the Paschal Mystery. "But where the Spirit of the Lord is, there is freedom" (2 Cor 3:17).

Notes for Chapter 3

1.
Andrew M. Greeley, "Fraternal Authority in the Church," *Homiletic and Pastoral Review*, 64 (1963-64), 561-570. Fr. Greeley's article evoked a number of interesting letters in the subsequent issues and also one article: T. Lincoln Bouscaren, S.J., "Fraternal Authority and Blind Obedience," *Homiletic and Pastoral Review*, 64 (1963-64), 921-925.

2.
Gregory Stevens, O.S.B., "Moral Obligation in St. Thomas," *The Modern Schoolman*, XL (1962), 3. Fr. Stevens summarizes in this article the renewal in Thomistic moral theology as enunciated by Deman and Tonneau.

3.
M. Huftier, "La loi ecclésiastique: Sa valeur et son obligation," *L'Ami du clergé*, 74 (1964), 375-382; Thomas E. Davitt, S.J., *The Nature of Law* (St. Louis: B. Herder, 1951).

4.
J. Tonneau, O.P., "Les lois purement pénales et la morale de l'obligation," *Revue des Sciences Philosophiques et Théologiques*, XXXVI (1952), 42.

5.
Summa Theologiae, II-II, q. 120, a. 1.

6.
Summa Theologiae, II-II, q. 120, a. 2.

7.
For an excellent summary of the teaching of contemporary theologians on epikeia, see Edouard Hamel, S.J., "La vertu d'épikie," *Sciences Ecclésiastiques*, 13 (1961), 35-56.

8.
Among the better English considerations of the nature of authority in the Church, see John L. McKenzie, S.J., "Authority and Power in the New Testament," *The Catholic Biblical Quarterly*, XXVI (1964), 413-422; John M. Todd, ed., *Problems of Authority* (Baltimore: Helicon Press, 1962); Yves M.-J. Congar, O.P., *Power and Poverty in the Church* (London: Geoffrey Chapman, 1964).

9.
Joseph Fuchs, S.J., "Auctoritas Dei in auctoritate civili," *Periodica de Re Morali, Canonica, Luturgica* LII (1963), 3-18.

10.
Summa Theologiae, II-II, q. 104, a. 1.

11.
For a partial summary of some recent literature on obedience, see Sister Teresa Mary, C.S.C., "Religious Obedience and Critical Thinking," *Review for Religious*, 22 (1963), 541-551.

12.
The crux of the problem revolves around the discernment of spirits. Contemporary theology must develop meaningful guidelines for the Christian striving to hear the voice of the Spirit. St. Paul always distinguishes the true Spirit in the light of charity, which is diametrically opposed to selfishness and seeking one's own personal whims. Charity seeks always to build up the unity of the Body of Christ in truth and love. Charity is also patient and long suffering. Cf., 1 Cor 12 and Eph 4.

13.
For a consideration of the prophetic office in the Church, see Karl Rahner, S.J., *The Dynamic Element in the Church* (London: Burns and Oates, 1964) . The trials and joys of the prophet are well described by Yves M.-J. Congar, O.P., "The Need for Patience," *Continuum*, 2 (1965) , 684-693.

Christian Marriage
and Family Planning

Chapter Four

I am a moral theologian. I teach in a seminary. Some nights I have trouble getting to sleep. Questions and doubts race through my mind about the Church's teaching on birth control. Every time I talk with other priests they invariably bring up the same subject. Why is birth control wrong? What shall we tell our penitents?

I think of a young couple I know who have nine children and live on a school teacher's salary. After their fourth baby a priest told them they had no reason to practice rhythm. He advised them to stay away from each other. But they *are* husband and wife. One day they came to tell me that the night before they had exchanged sexual intimacies; both were tense and he had lost the seed. Together they cried.

It seems to me that too often the Catholic attitude toward birth control is completely negative and that many Catholics also have a negative concept of Christian marriage. For them marriage means no divorce, no adultery and no birth control, period. Well, then, what is Christian marriage? First of all it is a sacrament, and a sacrament is a meeting, an embrace even, with Christ and God. The seven sacraments are seven different ways through which we can come into contact with God. In baptism we meet our heavenly Father through Christ our brother. In penance the sinner experiences the love and mercy of the forgiving Father. In holy orders a man shares in the unique priesthood of Christ, the one mediator of the new covenant. Under what aspect do husband and wife come into contact with God in matrimony?

God's love for man is a covenant, an alliance, that might be likened to a marital bond. The Old Testament is the story of God the lover, ever faithful to the alliance he made with Israel. God's fidelity and love reached their climax in the gift of his Son to redeem the world and inaugurate the new and permanent alliance of love between God and man.

In Christian marriage the love of husband and wife for each other shares and participates in the love of God for his people. Their reciprocal "yes" to one another is also a "yes" to the divine love of God. St. Paul tells husbands to love their wives as Christ loves his Church, and wives to love their husbands as the Church loves Christ, her spouse.

Like God's love for his people, the love of husband and wife is fertile, creative, life-giving. Every child they "create" is a permanent sign of the gift of love they have given to one another; this mutual love forms the school in which the child is educated and develops his natural and supernatural life; at the same time the mutual love of husband and wife fosters their own union with God. With this in mind it is perhaps easier to understand why the Church has always stressed that married love must be at the service of a generous procreation.

Sacred scripture gives a similar description of marriage. The older account of creation in Genesis (there are two accounts) mentions only the complementary, or loving, aspect of the relationship between Adam and Eve. The later account stresses the blessing of fruitfulness bestowed on Adam and Eve so that they might people the earth. Both scripture and the sacrament of matrimony show that marriage is a union of love in the service of life. Some might object that such a consideration of marriage is too theoretical, too ideal, too spiritual, typical of a poet or a celibate theologian. But I believe that many couples are living marriage in just that way.

For husband and wife their sanctity is in their mutual love and dedication to each other and to their family. Holiness is not synonymous with "fleeing the world." For married people it consists in their day by day imitation of Christ who gave his life for others. Husband and wife do not love God less because they love each other and their family. Did not Christ in one and the same act give himself perfectly to his Father and to all men?

Love is the cornerstone of marriage, yet theologians speak of love as a secondary end of marriage. It may be, however, that the problem of the ends of marriage and their mutual relationship is mostly a question of semantics. According to theologians like Leon Joseph Cardinal Suenens, Bernard Häring, Marc Oraison and Paul Anciaux, primary does not necessarily mean more important or possessing greater dignity; it simply means more specific. There are many unions of love—between brother and sister, among friends, that of a nun loving Christ her spouse. What distinguishes marriage from all other unions of love is that it is in the service of life, and specifically the life that is generated by the sexual union of husband and wife as the external expression of the union of their hearts. The *Constitution on the Church in the Modern World* wisely avoids the terminology of primary and secondary ends.

It should hardly be necessary to say that sex is good, because whatever is made by God is good. Still, it is undeniable that under the influence of heretics who proclaimed, at various times in the history of the Church, that all material things, especially sex, are evil, many Christian thinkers have taken an unduly pessimistic view of sex. Some Fathers of the Church, for example, linked sex and sexual pleasure with original sin: St. John Chrysostom thought that if it had not been for original sin, God would have provided a different means for procreation; St. Augustine believed there was venial sin in having marital relations except for the express purpose of procreation or in compliance with the request of one's spouse and then only to keep him (or her) from falling into sin. Today Christians generally have a more balanced and positive attitude toward sex, although in some places the older superstitions hang on. In any case, it should be clear that the sexual act recapitulates the gift of love that husband and wife have made to each other throughout the day.

The connection between sex and procreation is obvious. Love can be expressed in many other ways—a smile, a word, a kiss, a gift—but no other act could possibly be procreative. In giving man sexual organs God evidently had a procreative purpose. Therefore sex should be seen in its relation to the totality of marriage, the union of love in the service of life. Love demands that at times there be no sexual expression of it—in the weeks immediately preceding the birth of a child, for example, or when a wife, or husband, is ill. Some people object that any control or restriction of sex destroys the spontaneity of love, but all man's instincts must be under the control of reason. Love and its sexual expression must be a *personal* giving, not just an instinctive compulsion. It is through loving control that sex is assumed into the great reality of love. It is precisely here, in the deeply personal, specifically human relationship between love and sex that the Catholic teaching on control in marriage is rooted.

Sexual control is necessary for a practical reason, too, and that is that Christian couples should bring into the world only those children they can properly care for and educate as good Christians. Nor should they have so many children that they endanger their own spiritual, psychic or physical health. Human procreation is not merely biological; it must always be a reasonable expression of love. Therefore Catholic couples should prudently space their children over the entire span of their expected fertility.

How many children should a Catholic couple have then—two? four? six? Only a husband and wife, in prayerful dialogue with each other and with God, can answer that question for themselves because only they can decide the extent of their generous service to life. No priest or confessor can make the decision for them. The answer to the question—how many children—will vary with each couple. Generosity cannot be measured by numbers.

At the same time the situation is not as simple as it appears to those who say that since the Catholic Church believes in responsible parenthood, or birth control, there should be no quibbling over the means to achieve the desired goal; the simplest and most effective form of birth control should be used. But Catholic teaching opposes contraception, or artificial birth control, because it destroys the marital act as an expression of the union of love in the service of life. When any kind of barrier is placed between husband and wife, the sexual act no longer symbolizes the complete surrender of love. Something is held back. The act does not express the full gift of oneself to another, the gift of love. In contraception, man positively interferes with the sexual act so that it will not be open to procreation. Man can never achieve procreation on his own, of course. The existence of new life is a gift of God. Man merely performs an act that is open to procreation. It is precisely that openness which is eliminated in contraception.

In rhythm, man uses his knowledge of God's plan of nature in which a woman is only fertile during a short period in each menstrual cycle. Contraception asks for no control, no self-sacrifice. Rhythm does demand sacrifice; husband and wife cannot have relations whenever they want. The Church does not propose sacrifice for its own sake, however, but for the sake of a higher value. Love is the highest value in any marriage and the sacrifice of lesser pleasures and joys is a part of the gift of love. A contraceptive mentality can easily encase man in a world of sense that remains closed to any values higher than itself.

Christian asceticism, as it exists in marriage and out of it, is neither negative nor stoical. It is the daily living of baptism, dying to self and rising in the newness of life. The great paradox of Christianity is that it is only in losing that we find, only in giving that we receive, only in dying that we live. The cross never exists by or for itself. The cross is the way to the resurrection.

Whenever the birth control question is mentioned in mass media, television commentators or journalists invariably end by saying that everyone is looking forward to the day when science will provide a birth control pill that is cheap, safe, reliable and acceptable to people of all religions. The hope is not unreasonable, but we should nevertheless guard against the delusion that there are any simple, easy solutions to human problems. An efficient, cheap contraceptive in the bathroom cabinet will never solve the problems of marriage. Christians especially must never lose sight of the fact that we are pilgrims in this world, journeying toward eternity. The ultimate solution to human problems, including those of marriage, is the willingness of the Christian to imitate Christ, who gave his whole life to his Father and to all men.

Some Christians, however, seem to have fallen into the opposite error, leaving everything in the hands of divine providence. But God wants our cooperation in the work of building a new heaven and a new earth and so we must use technology and science in the service of the kingdom of God. Long ago Catholics should have been scientifically investigating the practice of rhythm. As it is, rhythm clinics are only now beginning to appear in Catholic dioceses. Through them and through continued research we may eventually arrive at a solution to the birth control problem. But even if that happens—and it cannot be stressed too often—marriage will always be a union of love in the service of life. The cross of Christ and his resurrection will continue to cast their shadow—and their light—on every marriage as on every human endeavor.

PRACTICAL APPLICATIONS

First of all, Catholic parents and teachers must develop in children a positive attitude toward sex as part of their education for marriage. In line with this, Catholic teaching and preparation for marriage ought to be rethought. There is infinitely more to living a Christian marriage than observing the three rules of no divorce, no adultery and no birth control. Building upon the virtue of chastity cultivated in adolescence, engaged couples should be helped to understand the need for sexual control in marriage. Too often they enter marriage with the best of intentions, but are totally unprepared for the problems and difficulties they will have to face. A young Catholic couple should try to avoid the predicament of having five children in five years, only to realize then that they should have no more children despite many more years of expected fertility.

A practical application for engaged girls would be for them to record their menstrual cycle, according to a medical director, for a year before marriage. The rhythm clinics now belatedly coming into existence should not limit their services to married women and mothers. They should be opened to single and engaged girls, too, so that they may be assisted in gathering and charting a record of from eight to thirteen cycles for the most effective use of rhythm. Should a girl become pregnant in the first months of marriage, she may never again have the opportunity to chart her cycles accurately. The time and bother connected with preparing for the practice of rhythm should be seen as an expression of the love of a girl for her future husband.

The effectiveness of the use of rhythm is, I realize, hotly debated among Catholics. Robert G. Potter, Jr., of Brown University, commented in the magazine, *Science* (March 27, 1964), that the effectiveness of rhythm "is not known precisely and perhaps never will be, since multiple forms of rhythm are in use and the motivation to practice it—or any method of contraception—effectively varies greatly depending on whether the couple are simply spacing a desired pregnancy or trying to prevent an unwanted one. The indications so far are that in average practice rhythm is less effective than such techniques as condom or diaphragm and jelly, but certainly it is nowhere near so ineffectual as implied. . . ." Potter cites other scientific studies that reach the same conclusion.

Dr. John Marshall, an English physician, in a recently published book, *The Infertile Period*, claims that "available figures do not suggest that the use of the infertile period is inferior to contraception." Dr. Marshall also rejects the assertion that the desire for sexual intercourse in women is most intense at the time of ovulation. It is interesting to note the sharp contrast between the balanced and carefully worded statements of these and other scientists with the hasty opinions aired by amateurs.

What about couples who are already married and find themselves in the midst of the problem of child spacing? When such people come to me for advice, I generally outline a four-point program.

1) Husband and wife must realize the supremacy of love and the necessity of manifesting their love in every possible way. In confession I often ask a woman what is her husband's favorite dessert. She is usually surprised by the question. She is even more surprised when I ask her if she would be willing to bake her husband's favorite cake as her penance. Such a penance is much more beneficial than mumbling a few prayers because it serves to remind a wife that her entire day is the living of the vow she made on her wedding day. I don't always find out the results of penances such as these, but one Sunday morning a man stopped me outside Church to say that he had just bought his wife a dishwasher. He never knew what a chore the dishes were until I had given him the penance of helping his wife with them.

2) A couple practicing rhythm are not expected to live as brother and sister. Even the strictest moralists permit "imperfect acts" between husband and wife. There are times when they feel the need to express their love in a sexual way; they do not intend to have complete sexual relations but merely sexual intimacies as an expression and sign of their love. If the husband comes to orgasm they need not complete the act if they have good reasons for not wanting another child at that time. It is not a sin.

In the past Catholics have put too much emphasis on the loss of seed, which is a purely physical-mechanical reaction. In itself, the loss of seed is neither good nor bad morally. Seed is lost in nocturnal emissions, or while swimming or horseback riding (a favorite example of 17th century moralists). In all these things the seed is lost *indirectly*, that is, the action was done for a reasonable purpose and not to bring about orgasm and the loss of seed. Is it not reasonable to allow (even at times urge) husband and wife to show their affection for each other through sexual intimacies even if orgasm might occur?

There is a danger of abuse in such a teaching, but it should be kept in mind that such a couple does not want or intend to have complete sexual relations, nor is there any consent to, or voluntary acceptance of, orgasm. They intend only what moralists call imperfect acts. To determine if love and fidelity are their true motives, the couple must consider their whole marital life. If in the other aspects of their life they are trying to live the union of love in the service of life, then their sexual affection and tenderness are a real expression of love, and not of selfishness.

Some people fear that such intimacies, especially on occasions when they indirectly result in orgasm, increase tensions between husband and wife because they do not reach a climax in a perfect union. On the contrary, when denied all sexual tenderness husband and wife tend to grow apart and release their sexual tendencies elsewhere—hobbies, hard work, or infidelity. Through the use of sexual intimacies they can express their love for one another even though they sacrifice the full sexual embrace. Indeed this sacrifice becomes part of their loving gift to one another.

3) Christian couples should aim at a gradual growth in self-control. Asceticism is necessary in every Christian life, but merely giving up something is not asceticism. We give up a good only for a greater good. Asceticism leads to the true freedom of the sons of God, who are free of the compulsion for any created good.

4) In the spiritual growth of husbands and wives, contact with the risen Christ in the sacraments is essential. Here the

Christian experiences the meaning and the reality of true love. In their sacramental embrace with Christ, husband and wife grow in their love for one another and for God.

I always stress that growth in self-control is a gradual process, especially for a couple in the habit of using artificial contraception. Those learning to grow in love and control will have some failures, but such acts are not subjectively sinful (they are due more to habit than to intention) *provided* the couple is making a sincere effort to improve. Ultimately, sin is not an external act but an interior state or disposition expressed in external acts. Couples must grow in their love and control; it will not come to them immediately or without prayer and effort.

The sin of artificial birth control committed by many couples today is not the traditional sin called "Onanism," which is characterized by a selfish attitude completely closed to the service of life. Many people practicing artificial contraception today have been and are generous in the service of life. More often than not, birth control today indicates a difficulty in integrating human sexuality into the whole personality.

Theologians and pastors must pay more than lip service to the moral principle of responsible parenthood. There are times when the health of a mother and the good of a family demand that the mother not become pregnant for the present. Under certain conditions it would be a greater evil to risk a pregnancy than to use contraceptives. Justice and charity toward wife and family prevail over chastity and the control of sexuality. Although artificial contraception is considered objectively wrong, there are times when, even objectively speaking, it is the lesser of two moral evils. Theologians admit that a confessor can counsel the lesser of two evils in a given situation.

Can the present teaching of the Church on birth control ever change? It *could* change, but that does not mean that it *will.* In any case, the teaching accepted in the church today is not directly a matter of faith. A few theologians, against the majority, believe that the teaching on contraception in the encyclical *Casti Connubii* is a defined matter of faith. Others maintain it is directly a matter of faith from the universal teaching of all the bishops of the Church. Such assertions are difficult to prove. The entire question is so complex that it is difficult to state, let alone prove. Any acquaintance with the historical evolution of the Church's teaching on marriage makes one wary of an argument against a change based on the universal teaching or magisterium.

In the official teaching of the Church, however, the condemnation of contraception (interfering with the conjugal act—e.g., a condom) is stronger and more solemn than the condemnation of sterilization (interfering with the generative faculty rather than with the act itself—e.g., ligating the tubes). The anovulant pill is mentioned only once in an official teaching—in an allocation of Pope Pius XII in September, 1958. According to the Pope, if such pills are taken for a contraceptive and not a therapeutic purpose, they are immoral. In matters such as these Catholics give an assent of *obedience*, not *faith*, to the teaching of the pope, unless the contrary can be proved.

Still, theologians have an obligation to ask questions. We owe it to our commitment to truth and to Catholic parents trying to live the Christian life. The very fact that a papal teaching on birth control is based on the natural law is an added reason for theologians to investigate further the natural law and its application in particular cases. Generally speaking, theological discussion should take place in theological journals, but on the subject of family planning, which affects so many Catholics directly, it seems necessary to assure Christian people that theologians *are* asking questions and at the same time to indicate their general tenor. But are married Catholics simply to sit back and wait for the answers? Not at all; most of them may not be able to solve theological problems, but they have much to tell theologians; they are, after all, *living* marriage day in and day out under the inspiration and guidance of the Holy Spirit. Theologians should be given the benefit of their experience, their insights and inspirations. A fruitful dialogue, however, requires restraint on both sides. Theologians should not disdain talking to married people who do not understand theology, and married couples should not dismiss theological principles as the mumblings of celibates.

The questions raised by theologians today concern especially the anovulant pill and the meaning of the principle of direct sterilization. Following Pope Pius XII, the current teaching on these questions involves two theological principles: totality and the twofold effect. The principle of totality maintains that the organs and parts of the body are immediately ordered to the good of the whole body and therefore can be sacrificed for the good of the whole. Thus, an infected arm or leg may be amputated for the good of the whole body.

The generative organs have a twofold finality: they are parts of the individual's body, but at the same time they have a social function and are ordered for another purpose, procreation. Man may interfere when the generative organs in their individual aspect are not functioning properly or are harmful for the whole body. For example, a doctor may remove a cancerous uterus even though the woman will become sterile as a result. Such a procedure is called an indirect sterilization: sterilization is an effect of the action, but not the effect intended by the doctor.

Man may not interfere for the good of the whole body when the generative aspect might be harmful for the whole body. For example, if pregnancy would cause heart trouble, the doctor may not ligate the tubes. Such a procedure is called direct sterilization because the sterilizing effect is intended as a means of preserving the mother's health. Referring to such cases, Pius XII said: "The danger appears only if voluntary sexual activity brings about a pregnancy that could threaten the aforesaid weak or diseased organs. The conditions that would allow the disposal of a part for the good of the whole by reasons of the principle of totality are lacking. It is therefore not morally permitted to interfere with the healthy tubes."

According to Pius XII, "By direct sterilization we mean an act whose aim is to make procreation impossible whether this is intended as a means or an end." The pope admitted that there are legitimate reasons for using anovulant pills, but, he went on, "a direct and, therefore, illicit sterilization results when ovulation is stopped to protect the uterus and the organism from the consequences of a pregnancy which it is not able to sustain. . . . It is likewise necessary to reject the view of a number of doctors and moralists who permit these practices when medical indications make conception undesirable. . . ."

The arguments against such a teaching have been advanced mainly by European theologians. Canon Louis Janssens of Belgium, in *Ephemerides Theologicae Lovanienses* (December, 1963), proposes an *ad hoc* argument. If the pill is direct sterilization, he says, so is rhythm. Intercourse at the infertile period aims to make procreation impossible. To the objection that in rhythm there is no positive interference with nature as there is in the pill, Canon Janssens replies that in rhythm time is employed as a contraceptive factor. What difference does it make, he asks, if space or time is used to avoid contraception? Furthermore, Janssens asserts, rhythm involves an even greater frustration of nature because a woman using it frustrates the ovum in every cycle. The pill does not waste the ovum but saves it for when a woman wishes it to be fecundated.

Louis Dupre, a lay theologian born in France, educated at Louvain and now teaching at Georgetown University, says in *Cross Currents* (Winter, 1964) that the natural law is dynamic and not static. He particularly questions the absolute value of the biological, procreational element in marriage. Individual acts by which man attains his end are not absolute, he insists. The procreational value does not exist in isolation but in relation to all the other values in the total complexity of man. In Dupre's view, all values are relativized by their relation to other values. One value cannot be extolled to the detriment of another value which is of equal or even greater importance.

Josef Maria Reuss is a German moral theologian and a bishop. In an article in *Tübinger Theologische Quartalschrift* (December, 1963) he stresses the necessary connection between love and procreation. Partnership and parenthood are mutually related, he says, but there are times when couples face a dilemma. For good reasons (health, finances, etc.) it may be wrong to have procreational copula at a particular time, yet love demands copula. If rhythm is ineffective, then man may interfere in the biological order for the good of the whole. Reuss believes that the question of how to interfere (pill, surgery, etc.) is a medical question and not a moral problem. Like Janssens, Reuss maintains that mechanical contraception is wrong because it prevents the act of sex from being a true expression of love. He also agrees that anovulant pills should not be used if rhythm is effective.

The Dutch theologian, W. van der Marck, O.P., in *Tijdschrift voor Theologie* (No. 4, 1963), says that the intention is the ultimate distinguishing feature of what constitutes direct sterilization. He develops (more at length than the others) the comparison with the question of the transplantation of organs. Traditionally, moralists have held that mutilation of the body is permitted for two reasons, curing the body or punishment. Then came the problem of organic transplantation. Some theologians believed that organic transplantation was wrong because it is a mutilation of the body which is neither a cure nor a punishment. The more common opinion today allows organic transplantation. The mutilation of oneself is specified by the intention of helping another human being. Van der Marck thinks that perhaps a third possibility, fertility control, might be added to the two uses of anovulant pills mentioned by Pius XII, namely, therapy or direct sterilization. The purpose of fertility control, Van der Marck says, specifies the taking of the pill so that it is neither sterilizing nor therapeutic. The fact that the end specifies the means is not the same as the unacceptable principle that the end justifies the means.

At the present time, such proposals are not sufficiently probable to follow in practice. Theologians, like scientists, must experiment constantly. Theological discussion and dialogue will test the validity of the arguments for and against the anovulant pills. The arguments thus far publicly advanced about them ultimately bring into question the notion of direct sterilization. The majority of all theologians today at least admit the need to refine the definition of direct sterilization proposed by Pius XII. (It is interesting, however, that the majority of those proposing new solutions admit that mechanical contraception is wrong because a contraceptive marital act ceases to be a symbol and manifestation of the total giving of love. Even so, theologians must further investigate, and question, the condemnation of contraception.)

Theologians today admit that a woman may use the pill for a contraceptive purpose if she is in danger of rape. Since in her case intercourse would not be voluntary, contraception would not be a frustration of nature. Another use involves a woman breastfeeding her baby. Some scientists claim that nature provides a natural protection against conception while a woman is nursing her child. In the stress and strain of modern life, however, "nature" does not always function properly. To correct this fact and ensure the sterility intended by nature, a nursing mother may take the pill.* Some theologians say a woman may take the pill from six to nine months after the birth of a child. But what about a mother who finds it impossible or difficult to nurse her child? Logically, she, too, should be allowed to use the pill.

There can be no frustration of nature in directly intending and provoking a sterilization when nature itself "wants" a woman to be sterile. But how do we know when nature "wants" sterility? From the health and condition of the genital organs alone or from the lack of some biological element that should be present? The genital organs do not exist in a vacuum. They belong to particular persons in particular circumstances at particular times. If nature does not "want" a woman to conceive, can we interfere with nature to induce sterility? Or, must the woman and her husband simply abstain from marital relations? Pius XII did consider such cases and he concluded that the principle of totality does not apply to them.

It remains to be asked why is the physical integrity of the marital act normative? Theologians generally reply that the marital act by its very definition is the depositing of male semen in the vagina of the woman. What value or meaning does such a norm preserve? It is true that the norm of physical integrity of the marital act and the control demanded by it help to ensure that sexual communication is an expression of love and not primarily a selfish seeking after sexual pleasures. But is there not a more qualitative and personal norm

---

*Some doctors believe this practice may harm the infant.

to ensure that sexuality is an expression of love? Cannot conscientious Christian couples best judge the meaning of their intimate sexual union? Are there any other values that are protected by the norm of physical integrity of the marital act?

Even more complex considerations underlie the problems I have raised—the concept of the natural law, the nature of human sexuality, the ends of marriage. Just as medical scientists continue to investigate possible harmful effects of the pill and to seek ways of detecting the precise time of ovulation, or even of inducing it, so too, theologians must continue to ask questions and seek answers. Nevertheless, if it is unscientific not to ask questions, it is demagoguery to raise false hopes.

One thing is certain. No pill or change in teaching will open the gates of heaven. Men will always know sorrow, suffering, difficulties and problems. We are pilgrims traveling to a new heaven and a new earth. Christ is our hope. Our free response to God's love will be to live the redeeming Paschal mystery of Christ—dying to self and rising in the newness of life.

In this chapter I have tried to express as cogently as possible the rationale behind the present teaching of the Church on birth control and at the same time to indicate the possibility of a change in the teaching. Chapter Five presents some theological arguments which seem to justify the need for a change. Chapter Seven examines both the concept of the natural law and the teaching authority of the Church to show that a change in the teaching on birth control would be compatible with the teaching office of the living Church. I hope that the development in my own thinking as expressed in these three chapters will be indicative of the development in the official magisterium of the Church.

Personal Reflections on Birth Control

Chapter Five

Between the previous chapter, written about a year earlier, and the present one, I have added my own "Amen" to those who are asking for a change in the present teaching of the Church. Why the change?

My arguments in favor of the present teaching of the Church developed along the lines of the controlling and directing influence of love with regard to sexuality. The present teaching of the Church emphasizes the dignity and spiritual freedom of man who controls and determines his whole life. The spiritual core of man guides and gives intelligibility to the material part of human nature. Contraception, by not directly appealing to the higher forces of love and control, could easily enclose man in the realm of the purely material. Sacrifice and control will always be a part of man's life. True

Christian asceticism does not constrain the individual; rather it enables the Christian to participate ever more in the freedom of the children of God which only the life-giving Spirit can produce. Like Christ, man dies to self and rises in the newness of life.

A brief reflection shows that the position outlined above is more of a defense than an argument. The reasoning assumes the present teaching of the Church and then tries to explain it within the whole context of the Paschal Mystery which is the basis of all Christian life. But theologians cannot merely assume the truth of the present teaching of the Church. Is such love and control an essential element of Christian marriage?

EXPERIENCE OF MARRIED COUPLES

Contact and dialogue with many married Christians forced me to reconsider my views. Many couples found themselves in the dilemma of realizing a need to express their love in a human way and yet dared not have any more children. Family love and marriages were weakened and at times almost destroyed because couples could not fully express their love in a sexual way. The question arose almost instinctively—would such a couple be breaking their relationship with God by using contraception? In some cases I was sure that the couple would not be guilty of mortal sin.

Some had taken the risk and decided to use contraception. Many other conscientious non-Catholic Christians are doing the same. Are they breaking their relationship with God? How can I tell? The criterion frequently proposed in scripture is the love of our neighbor. How can we love the God we do not see if we cannot love our neighbor whom we do see? The last judgment as portrayed in Matthew's account bases man's relationship with God on his relationship with his fellow men. "For when I was hungry, you gave me food; when thirsty, you gave me drink. . . ." (Matt 25:31-46) . Some people using contraception are most generous in their love of God and neighbor. A good number have followed the teaching of the Church, but now find that their marriage, their health, and their finances persuade them not to have any more children. They are devoted husbands and wives, fathers and mothers; they give of their few moments of free time in projects for the betterment of society; they are kind to all; they go out of their way to help others; they try to overcome their feelings of vengeance and rancor. By their fruits you will know them. They seem to be good Christians who have not broken their relationship with God.

Theologians have always admitted that something can be objectively sinful even though for a particular person because of subjective circumstances it might not be a subjective sin. But the frequency of the subjective occurrence does raise doubts about the objective sinfulness. My attention focused on three aspects connected with the present teaching of the Church: human sexuality, the nature of the moral judgment, the authority and teaching of the popes.

HUMAN SEXUALITY

Does the present teaching of the Church reflect the complex reality of human sexuality? Through their sexual union husband and wife express and intensify their union of love. Three influences—comparatively recent medical knowledge, various theological aberrations, and a celibate attitude toward sexuality—have tended to give a rather distorted notion of sexuality.

For centuries the lack of biological and medical knowledge made it impossible for man to separate procreation and sexuality. St. Alphonsus, the 18th century patron of moral theologians and confessors, followed the biological concepts of Aristotle and Galen. The uterus was the nest in which the child developed. The woman contributed certain fluids or even a type of semen which mixed with the male semen in the uterus, coagulated, became frothy, and evolved into the embryo. New scientific discoveries, aided by the invention of the microscope, expanded medical knowledge in the late seventeenth century. For example, de Graaf proposed the evidence that the female testes are ovaries, and he described the follicles that ever since have been associated with his name. Only with the work of Ogino and Knaus (1929-1930) did man become certain of the comparatively short time in a female cycle when a woman is fertile. Until 100 years ago, inadequate medical knowledge led theologians to believe that every sexual union was connected with the real possibility of procreation. The science of theology in accepting the theological principles of older theologians has also, perhaps unconsciously, accepted a rather one-sided concept of sexuality.

The theological aberrations of Gnosticism, Jansenism, and all others that look down on the material part of man have tended to overemphasize the procreative aspect of sexuality. For many centuries it was the intention of procreation which alone completely justified marital intercourse. Theories proposing the evil of matter concentrate on sexuality. Many zealots falsely interpreted the Pauline dichotomy of flesh and spirit in an ontological sense as the war between the spiritual and the material in man. Today theology has a renewed consciousness of the value of earthly realities. Matter is not bad; it is a part of the order of creation and the order of the redemption through the Paschal Mystery. Sexuality no longer appears as an evil which is tolerated for the purpose of procreation.

My own celibacy puts me at a disadvantage in considering

marital sexuality. There is no experimental knowledge of the meaning of sexuality in marriage. In addition, a celibate mentality can easily form a warped concept of sexuality in marriage. I too was trained in the idea that the pleasures of sex make up for the burdens of marriage. Masturbation thus appears as the starting point for a theology of marital sexuality! Even though I reject such a concept of sexuality, I have still been influenced by it. A celibate attitude does tend to see sexuality only in the light of pleasure and procreation.

Today theologians acknowledge the love-union aspect of marital sexuality. In fact, the love-union aspect of sexuality "justifies" marital sexuality when procreation is impossible. With the acceptance of rhythm, it seems that the Church has admitted the love-union value of sexuality as a value in its own right apart from procreation. Seen in such a light, contraception does not differ that much from rhythm. It is true that sexuality must always be an expression and intensification of love, but conscientious husbands and wives should know best the demands of love in their own lives.

THE MORAL JUDGMENT

The moral judgment is the final and ultimate judgment, reducing, as it were, all the other aspects of the question. The moral judgment presupposes all the other considerations bearing on a particular problem—the sociological, psychological, pedagogical, hygienic, etc. Every other consideration is partial and particular with regard to the moral consideration. The moral judgment considers all the various aspects and then arrives at its final judgment. In most moral judgments some particular value (not a moral one as such) might have to be sacrificed for the good of the whole. Nothing in this world is perfect from every conceivable point of view. Every other aspect of the problem is relative to the final moral judgment. What if the biological integrity of the marital act destroys such other considerations as the educational, the love union of the spouses, the psychic and physical health of the spouses?

It seems that only in our own times has the consideration of biological integrity interfered with the other aspects that enter into the final moral judgment. Previously the cruel forces of disease and famine made the problem of family planning much less acute. Likewise, an agrarian culture was more in keeping with larger families than our highly industrialized civilization. The formation and growth of Planned Parenthood in the present century indicate that the recognition of the problem of family planning has come about only recently. Catholic theologians have popularized the expression "responsible parenthood" only in the last decade. Perhaps in earlier times the biological integrity of the marital act did not interfere with other values. But today the biological integrity must be considered together with the love-union aspect of sexuality, the health of the partners, the proper education of the children, and demographic circumstances. The biological aspect is not an absolute; it is a partial and relative consideration in the process of formulating the final moral judgment.

TEACHING OF THE CHURCH

As human beings we experience our own inadequate knowledge and the selfish promptings from the effects of original sin in us. Man realizes his need for guidance and direction. On the other hand, the teaching authority of the Church on birth control is not infallible, not a matter of faith. The condemnation of contraception belongs to the ordinary, authentic magisterium of the Church to which we owe obedience. The very fact that the Church has not spoken infallibly indicates that the present teaching is open to development.

To change the present teaching of the Church would be a case of development and not a direct contradiction. Gregory Baum has compared a development on the birth control issue with the development of the Church's teaching on religious liberty (*Contraception and Holiness,* New York: Herder and Herder, 1964, pp. 311-343) . The encyclicals of Pius IX and Leo XIII condemn religious liberty because of the false principles on which it is based. Pope John in *Pacem in Terris* and the Council Fathers of Vatican II have approved religious liberty. The Church still condemns the false basis of religious liberty proposed in the last century. However, the Church has recently become more conscious of the freedom of conscience of the individual in religious matters. The inviolability of the human person from external force and the freedom of the act of faith are the bases of the individual's freedom in matters of religion. The teachings of Pope John and the Council Fathers are not a contradiction but a development of the earlier teaching.

Another example: the encyclical *Mediator Dei* (1947) teaches that, "His cruel sufferings constitute the mystery from which our salvation chiefly springs." The *Constitution on the Sacred Liturgy* teaches that the Paschal Mystery is the heart of the redemption. The constitution on the liturgy reflects the theological, scriptural, and liturgical rediscovery of the resurrection in the plan of redemption. Pius XII in 1947 only reflected the thought of his own day, but there has been a growth in our understanding of the resurrection in the past two decades.

The present teaching of the Church on birth control reflects the theological consciousness of the Church at the time it was formulated. Since *Casti Connubii* (1930) the theology of the Church has given more attention to the love-union aspect of sexuality. The bitter controversy over the licitness of rhythm in the 1930's shows that the whole church at that time did not have an adequate understanding of the love-union aspect of sexuality as a value in itself, completely apart from the possibility of procreation. Only in the last decade have theologians talked about the principle of responsible parenthood. Pius XI probably never heard of such a principle. The present teaching of the Church reflects the connection between sexuality and procreation. The project of marriage will always be procreative. But it does not seem that the present teaching of the Church reflects the demands of responsible parenthood and the love-union aspect of sexuality.

A consideration of three ideas—sexuality, the moral judgment, and the teaching authority of the Church—have influenced me to change my thinking on the present teaching of the Church on contraception. The question completely transcends the discussion about the pill. Those who advocate the use of the pill generally argue within the framework of the same categories that theologians have used with regard to marital sexuality. Now the Church must reconsider the categories and principles themselves. The proposal to change the present teaching of the Church on contraception is not a capitulation to situation ethics and a denial of any objectivity. Moral theology today does need a more personalist approach. But the proposal for a change is based on the need for a more exhaustive, objective consideration. I do not believe that the present teaching of the Church properly reflects all the objectivity in the complex reality of marital sexuality.

Both the thought and tone of the present essay are personal. I have not attempted to give a scientific and detailed argumentation; rather, I have tried to show why I have changed my own thinking. Pope Paul has pointed out the complexity and the gravity of the problem. The Pope concluded his statement by saying, "And therefore it seems opportune to recommend that no one, for the present, takes it on himself to make pronouncements in terms different from the prevailing norm." The present essay is in no way a pronouncement; it is a highly personal reflection. Nor am I advocating in practice a norm "different from the prevailing norm." My own rethinking of the subject only makes me more aware of my own limitations and less prone to make any pronouncements whatsoever.

IN PRACTICE

As a confessor and guide I must continue to uphold the present teaching of the Church. In and through their marriage a Christian couple must live the gift of the Paschal Mystery. Married Christians are not second class citizens; they are called to perfection. I stress the primacy of love in their lives. In giving marriage instructions I will spend the entire first talk on the Sermon on the Mount with its emphasis on love of others and dying to self.

The counsellor should suggest practical ways of showing marital love; e.g., the husband comes home from work and, instead of burying himself in the paper or TV screen, takes the time to share his day with his wife. Love is the most important element in their marriage. Their sexual union must be an expression and intensification of their union of love in the service of life. Young couples should be reminded of the need for responsible parenthood. I point out that rhythm with the help of a competent doctor and the use of the thermometer is more reliable than many people believe. But it is a real sacrifice for a woman trying to take her temperature when she first awakens and the children are crying and/or fighting in their bedroom. Love becomes very practical on occasion.

However, it could be that in a particular case for a particular couple in their individual circumstances the use of contraceptives might not break their relationship with God. Theologians have always admitted that in certain circumstances there might not be subjective guilt. Chancery officials today frequently imply that suicides are not guilty of grave sin. No confessor believes that all the acts of masturbation confessed by adolescents are subjectively serious sins. A couple might come to the conclusion that in their particular circumstances contraception is needed to preserve very important values in their lives.

The ultimate judgment must always be made by the individual couple. I try to see from their whole life if they have broken their relationship with God. I apply the criteria mentioned in first part of the essay with regard to their relationships with one another, with their family, their fellow workers, their neighbors, and their enemies. The fact they have made a real effort in the past would argue for their good faith. I encourage them to continue building up their relationship with God and each other. The decision to use contraception is difficult and risky. The danger of self-deception is ever present, but there are times when contraception might be necessary for an individual couple. I have counselled couples along these lines.

The complexity of the problem of birth control is evident. Since my consideration of the problem has completely neglected many aspects of the question, I dare not make any pronouncements. We must all admire the wisdom of the Pope in setting up a special commission to investigate the varied aspects of the teaching of the Church on marriage. But we must also recognize the complex circumstances that enter into the judgment made by an individual couple.

Natural Law and the Teaching Authority of the Church

Chapter Six

The present discussion about the teaching of the Catholic Church on birth control has focused on two primary issues—the question of natural law and the teaching authority of the Church. Although a full treatment of natural law is impossible within a few pages, some clarifications would be most helpful.

Too often in the past Catholic writings have implied that the natural law consists in detailed norms and exact rules for human conduct. Such is not the case. Confusion arises from our own legalistic understanding of the word law. For St. Thomas law means an order of reason, a plan, a design. Hence the natural law means the plan or design according to which human life should be lived. Undoubtedly an older philosophy conceived of human existence in more static terms as conformity to a pre-arranged plan that was spelled out in every detail. Man's experience of the world in which he lives shapes his philosophy. Primitive man was so fascinated by nature and its powers that he frequently made nature his God. Man before the last few centuries was powerless to bring about any change in nature. His happiness consisted merely in trying to conform his life to the patterns of nature and reality. Greek philosophy that talked about a pre-existing world of ideas also put the primary emphasis on the conformity of things in this world to the already existing world of ideas.

Modern man thinks of the world and nature not as something static but dynamic; creativity and invention, not conformity, characterize modern man. Technological and scientific progress has changed our whole outlook on reality and the world. Contemporary man does not bow down before nature and conform his life to the pattern of nature. The twentieth century man rolls up his sleeves and goes to work to shape nature according to his plans. Creativity, growth and progress are the bywords of our life. Bulldozers change the face of the terrain; scientists are trying to plan the weather that man will enjoy; technology has overcome the problems of inertia and gravity so that men in today's world can even fly to the moon; computers have completely revolutionized our approach to certain problems; the theory of evolution has changed our static image of the world. Is it any wonder that modern man refuses to listen to a natural law proposed as mere conformity to the laws of nature? Rather I look upon natural law as a task to be achieved, a God-given destiny to be worked out and developed. The moral life of man like his physical and psychological life is characterized by growth and development.

Catholic theology must also face up to another reality. The natural law, at least until the time of Thomas, was not a coherent ethical system about which all Catholic thinkers were in unanimous agreement. In St. Thomas' writings on natural law he gives at least four other definitions in addition to his own. These earlier definitions, proposed by Cicero, the famous Roman philosopher; Ulpian, the Roman jurist; St. Isidore of Seville; and Gratian, the monk who first collected the laws of the Church, differ quite a bit among themselves.

In the matter of marriage and procreation the definition of Ulpian is most significant. According to Ulpian, the natural law is what nature teaches all the animals—what man has in common with all the other animals such as the physical union of the sexes, the education of offspring, etc. Using such a definition of the natural, Thomas and most theologians when treating the sins against chastity or the sixth commandment make a twofold division—sins against nature and sins according to nature. That is right—there are sins according to nature! Since nature is that which is common to all animals, in matters of sexuality it means the physical union of male and female. Homosexuality would be against such a concept of nature, but fornication and adultery would be according to nature. This is the most striking indication that not all Catholic thinkers are in agreement about the definition of nature. There is a very important meaning behind the term natural law, but natural law does not designate a monolithic philosophical system. The basic understanding of natural law is that God has endowed man and the world with an evolving being and human life must develop according to its God given reality.

In addition, notice the concept of man that follows from Ulpian's definition of the natural law. Man is composed of two layers—a bottom layer of animality which he shares with all animals and a top layer of rationality. But the rationality as it were just fits on the top and does not penetrate the animality. Whatever belongs to animality cannot be changed or interfered with by rationality. But does not human greatness mean that man by his reason can control and integrate his whole human life? (St. Thomas does mention and even stresses this aspect, but I do not think he ever completely integrated it into Ulpian's definition of the natural law.) Many people believe that the concept of the natural law has been too biological precisely because of this two-layer vision of man. In matters other than procreation man frequently does interfere with the "natural" order.

Often we receive the impression that the Church has come to its teaching about particular moral issues by arguing from a natural law theory. I have the suspicion that in many cases the reality is just the opposite. The Church teaches a particular point because it seems to be a part of the scriptures and the living tradition of the Church. Confronted with the teaching of the Church on particular issues, theologians then try to construct a system to show that such a teaching is most logical and meaningful. Since natural law was known both to Greek philosophy and Roman law, it became an excellent tool to rationalize (in the good sense of the term) and explain coherently the Church's teaching. I do not think that in her moral teaching, at least for the greater part of her existence, the Church has proceeded from a theoretical understanding of natural law to practical conclusions about moral conduct. Rather the natural law has been used to buttress and support existing teachings.

In a real sense any philosophical system, especially any philosophical notion supporting a revealed doctrine, starts out with certain given facts and then tries to explain them in a coherent manner. The value of any such system depends on whether it does correspond to reality as experienced. In their effort to give a reasonable explanation of the particular teaching of the Church on a given question, Catholic thinkers have tried to show that such a teaching is a dictate of nature and shares in the immutability of nature. Man always tends to find as much support as he can for his own way of looking at reality. Do we not all strive to make our position as strong as we can by bringing in all possible arguments? Basically the question narrows down to the problem of what came first—the particular teaching or the so-called system. I am sure that on some occasions, especially more recent ones, Catholic thinking has gone from the system to the practical conclusion. But precisely because the natural law even today is not a coherent system in which agreement reaches down to all the particulars, I believe that in many matters the theory of natural law is used to support and explain existing teachings.

I do believe there is a basic truth in natural law theory that must be preserved. Morality can never become a matter of whim or caprice, but must always correspond to reality. Man must develop the existence and life that God has given to him. Man through his reason can know in general the meaning of his existence and how he must live it. However, I do not believe that the natural law is a code or even a matter of static conformity. Nor do I believe that the natural law has been (at least for the greater part of the Church's existence) a detailed and harmonious system. Finally, I think natural law has been used more often to explain already existing teaching rather than as a theory to propose particular moral norms.

The above observations about natural law are tentatively proposed. Not all would agree with them. However, there seems to be a growing consensus today among theologians that the natural law arguments with regard to the present teaching of the Church on birth control are not absolutely conclusive. Even those who defend the present teaching (e.g., Fr. Kelly, Fr. Ford, Dr. John Marshall) admit that the natural law arguments do not seem absolutely certain. Consequently, many agree that the real point at issue in the birth control controversy is the teaching authority of the Church.

One who argues for a change in the Church's policy must show how such a change would be compatible with the teaching mission of the Church. The following situations well illustrate the problems, both theoretical and practical, that anyone who favors change must answer.

Usually after a lecture or talk, there is an embarrassing pause while the speaker anxiously awaits a hesitant hand to signal a question or comment. One night after giving a talk in which I argued for a change in the present teaching of the Church, I experienced no embarrassing pause in waiting for a question. As the question period opened a man quickly sprang to his feet. "For twenty years my wife and I have been making many sacrifices to live according to the teaching of the Church on marriage and birth control. We have lived with frustration, financial hardship, sickness, and even the threat of death. I am sure there are millions of loyal Catholics like us. It would be totally unfair to us if the Church ever changed its teaching."

An older theologian once said to me: "Father, I was ordained by the Church to bring God to men and men to God. I have always tried to be a loyal priest and theologian. On platforms and stages in every part of this country I have explained and defended the teaching of the Church on birth control. Do you mean to tell me that by being loyal to the Church I have placed an unnecessary burden on innumerable Catholic couples? Think of all my students who are now hearing confessions. Instead of helping to bring men to God, have I put an obstacle in their path? How could God ever allow such a thing to happen to his Church and to his loyal priests, theologians, and married couples?"

Others fear that any change in the teaching of the Church

on birth control would destroy the whole teaching office of the Church. If the Church is wrong on birth control, it can also be wrong in other matters.

CHANGE IS POSSIBLE

Despite all the serious objections, a change in the teaching of the Church on contraception is possible. (Note that in speaking about change I refer both to "the pill" and other forms of contraception in general. The teaching of the Church is much stronger with regard to contraception in general, but here too I believe that change is also necessary.) Although the teaching on contraception is found in papal encyclicals, such a teaching is not infallible. Responsible theologians in the Church are arguing for a change. A few Fathers of the Vatican Council and bishops of the Church have publicly expressed their desire for change. The very fact that the Pope set up his famous commission shows that in his mind change is possible. I grant that at the beginning the question confronting the commission probably concerned just "the pill." I grant that the Pope admitted "that as of now we do not have sufficient reason to regard the norms given by Pius XII as surpassed and therefore not binding." But the Pope did admit there was a problem to be studied: "We know indeed how exceedingly delicate and full of responsibility is the mission we have entrusted to you. There is a problem which deeply interests public opinion and which rightly worries married couples and their pastors." One must conclude from the above evidence that change is possible.

But what about the serious objections mentioned above? There will never be any clear-cut answers to such objections, but perhaps I can give some helpful reflections. First, what about the married man's reaction that change would be unfair to him and all the other Catholics who have sacrificed so much to live according to the present teaching of the Church? A few days after hearing that objection, I came across the scriptural parable of the owner of the vineyard (Matt 20:1-16). At various times during the day, the owner went out to hire men to work in his vineyard. At the end of the day he paid them all the same amount—one day's wage. Those who had worked under the hot sun of the day for twelve hours complained that it was unjust to pay them the same amount as those who had worked for only one hour in the cool of the evening. Such treatment is not fair; it is unjust. The owner responded, "Have I not a right to do what I choose? Or art thou envious because I am generous?"

The parable of the vineyard reminded me of the parable of the prodigal son (Luke 15:11-32). The elder son could not understand how his father could forgive his brother. "Behold these many years I have been serving thee, and have never transgressed one of thy commands; and yet thou hast never given me a kid that I might make merry with my friends. But when this thy son comes who has devoured his means with harlots, thou hast killed for him the fattened calf." I am not blaming the man who made the objection that any change in the teaching on birth control would be unfair, but there does seem to be a parallel between his objection and the objections raised by the workers in the vineyard.

A second reflection: the wisdom of God is evident in many changes both inside and outside the Church. Fifty years ago many people died of T.B.; today thanks to medical advances T.B. is no longer a killing disease. Today many people are dying of cancer. Perhaps in the future medicine will be able to cure cancer with a simple pill. Is God unjust because some people are suffering and dying today who would not have to suffer and die if they lived in the next century?

DEVELOPMENT OF DOCTRINE

But is development and change possible in the Church? I am convinced that St. Peter would probably flunk a third grade religion exam. Peter could not answer the questions about the Persons in God or the number of sacraments. Only gradually did the Church develop and formulate its teaching on the Persons in God and the sacraments. But has the Church ever changed its teaching on moral issues? Papal encyclicals in the nineteenth century denied religious liberty. Today the Vatican Council has proclaimed religious liberty.

Can the Church, however, change on a matter that is so closely connected with mortal sin and eternal salvation? The Church has changed its discipline on a very important matter affecting eternal salvation—the sacrament of penance. During the first six centuries Christians could receive the sacrament of penance only once. Consequently, Christians put off the celebration of penance until near death. Today Christians can celebrate the sacrament of penance as often as they wish. Obviously many people of the first six centuries were deprived of a most important opportunity. Was the Church wrong for such a long period of time? Was God unjust and unfair in so vitally important a matter? There are no answers to these questions. Whenever the divine wisdom and election are called into question, all we can do is to respond with St. Paul who answered a similar complaint by saying, "O man, who are thou to reply to God?" (Rom 9:20) .

A third reflection: any change would be a development and not a contradiction of the past. We have mentioned that Papal encyclicals in the nineteenth century condemned religious liberty, whereas the Vatican Council has proclaimed religious liberty. The Church condemned religious liberty in the past because of the false bases of religious liberty—laicism, secularism, relativism, and indifference. Today the Church bases its teaching on the dignity of the human person. So too in matters of marriage and sexuality, the Church is much more conscious today of the love-union aspect of sexuality and the need for responsible parenthood. The present teaching of the Church recognizes the need for a generosity in procreation, but does the teaching of the Church reflect the present awareness of the love-union aspect of sexuality and the need for responsible parenthood? Since the Church has become more conscious of other values involved in marriage, its teaching can develop in the light of a greater awareness of such values.

A fourth reflection: the Church is the people of God—not just the hierarchy. I do not think that a change with regard to birth control would destroy the meaning and effectiveness of the Church. In fact, there could be no better illustration of the teaching of the Vatican Council that the Church is the people of God. Personally, I changed my own thinking on birth control because of many contacts with married couples. The clamor for change in the Church originated with married couples who are trying to live the Christian life. The Church can and does learn from the experience of Christians living their lives under the inspiration of the Holy Spirit.

The possibility of a change in the teaching of the Church on responsible parenthood forces theologians to reconsider the entire question of the authoritative teaching of the Church. Our discussion will center on just one point—how does the Church arrive at its moral teaching on a given point? The basis for all the teaching of the Church must be sacred scripture. On some matters, however, the scriptures are not as clear as one might wish; for example, in the matter of marriage and divorce there is a problem of interpreting the text of Matthew 19:9. Scripture seems to contain outright condemnations of oaths and interest, but the Church today uses oaths and allows the taking of interest. All the more reason why the Church must interpret the Word of God and keep it living. On the question of contraception the only possible direct reference comes from the account of Onan in Genesis, but scripture scholars today do not believe that the text is a convincing proof against contraception. There seems to be nothing explicit in scripture about contraception; but even if there were passages, they would need interpretation.

Does the Church reason to all its teachings under the inspiration of the Holy Spirit? As already mentioned, the Church in many areas does not start from a theory of natural law and then proceed to conclusions. When the teaching on contraception was first enunciated I am sure it was not the result of a theoretical and philosophical system. Even today there appears to be doubt about the natural law arguments.

What about the tradition of the Church? The tradition and constant teaching of the Church are most important. But a difficulty arises when we realize that the traditional teaching of the Church on some points in the past has changed; for example, religious liberty, usury, cooperation with other religions, the love-union value of marriage and marital sexuality, the concept of servile work as a violation of the meaning of Sunday. Why the change? Obviously changing times and circumstances played a great part. But there is another element that enters into the teaching of the Church which is frequently forgotten—the living experience of the Christian people. In all the examples mentioned above the experience of Christian people seems to have been the primary factor in the change of the traditional teaching. The Holy Spirit is the primary teacher in the Church, but the Spirit does teach in the lives of the faithful in whom he dwells.

If Christian experience is so important, what is going to happen to the teaching authority of the Church? If individual experience is the ultimate criterion, is the door not opened for pure subjectivism and anarchy? I do not think so. The Church must always teach and proclaim the basic values of the Christian life. The Church with its long memory (tradition) has learned much and imparts this wisdom to her children. Individual Christians, however, nourished by the Church and given life by the Holy Spirit will have to reconcile those values which because of changing times might come into conflict. Again, all the more reason for the teaching authority of the Church. The Church represents the collective conscience and experience of all her children. A particular person might be prejudiced and wrong, but the teaching Church must judge in the light of her own traditions and the collective experience of her living members.

Change then will often happen from underneath. Certain individuals will begin to clamor for change. The Church will have to test their claims and then finally render her judgment. Change in the Church frequently results from what theology now calls the prophetic office in the Church. Just as in the Old Testament, so too now God continues to raise up prophets to teach and instruct his Church. Here too there lies the great danger of false prophets. Some people have gone too far and become heretical, but others have been influential in having the Church change her understanding and teaching. Theology badly needs to develop a consideration of the prophetic office and the ways for discerning the true prophets in the Church. Frequently only in retrospect can we discover the true prophets. Since the magisterial or teaching Church reflects the experience of Christian people, on some occasions the teaching Church will be behind the times.

Many practical problems remain. Has the Church always been wrong in the many areas of change? When does something stop being wrong and become right? What about the people who have been acting against the official teaching of the Church? What if the Church does not change its official teaching on birth control? I just cannot give an answer to these questions; in fact, there are no pat answers for such questions. Perhaps in the past the Church has too often tried to play God by having a ready answer for everything. Perhaps the Church has not really trusted in the life-giving power and teaching role of the Holy Spirit. Undoubtedly at times we have tried to trap the Holy Spirit in our institutions and laws. However, from an understanding of change in the Church all must realize the importance of the experience of the Christian people in forming the teaching of the Church. Change always implies stress, strain, and difficulties. Change in the Church is no different. The Vatican Council constantly reminds us of the pilgrim Church, but a truly pilgrim Church will always know and experience the problem of change and growth.

The commission established by the Pope is an excellent illustration of the way in which the teaching authority of the Church functions. The Pope called the commission together to study the problem from all different angles. Among those chosen were married couples, so that the whole Church might profit from their experience. The teaching authority of the Church is attuned to the voice of the Spirit, but the Holy Spirit also speaks in the lives of those Christians in whom he dwells.

A change in the teaching of the Catholic Church on birth control is possible. I do not think that a change would jeopardize the faith of Catholics or the teaching mission of the Church. In fact, a change in the present teaching on birth control would serve to give us a much better insight into the mystery of the Church.

The Mixed Marriage
Promises

Chapter Seven

According to the present discipline of the Church (canons 1061 and 1071), the *cautiones* are required for the validity of the dispensation in a case of mixed marriage or disparity of cult. The *cautiones* in the universal law of the Church are two promises: (1) the non-Catholic party gives a guarantee to remove from the Catholic party the danger of perversion of faith; and (2) both parties give a guarantee that all offspring will be baptized and reared only in the Catholic faith. Canon 1060 states that mixed marriages are forbidden by divine law itself where there is danger of perversion of the faith of the Catholic spouse or the children. The *cautiones* are the means established by Church law to remove the danger of perversion.

The point at issue is not what form the *cautiones* should

take, but the question, does divine law demand that the promises be made in any form? With regard to the first promise, the danger of perversion for the Catholic spouse, there is no great problem. Both parties could agree to respect and mutually enhance their Christian faith. In the case of marriage with a non-baptized person both parties could agree to respect the conscience of the other and work for their mutual development and fulfillment. Such promises would not be offensive to either of the parties and would be consonant with the principles of religious liberty.

The crux of the problem is to raise all the children of the marriage in the Catholic faith. Does divine law demand that all the children be raised in the Catholic faith?

THE HISTORICAL ARGUMENT

One could argue from history that it has not always been so. St. Paul did not absolutely forbid marriages with a pagan (1 Cor 7:12-16), although he forcefully pointed out the difficulties involved (2 Cor 6:14). Some early councils prohibited marriages with pagans, but it was not until the twelfth century that the sanction of nullity appeared. The present canonical legislation with regard to the canonical form, the impediments of mixed religion and disparity of cult, as well as the *cautiones* themselves, appeared comparatively late in the history of the Church.[1]

Likewise, even in the last century in certain countries in mixed marriages the boys have been raised in the religion of the father and the girls in the religion of the mother. Or every other child has been raised in the Catholic faith. It is a historical fact that the Church was not always aware of the divine obligation to raise the children of mixed marriages in the Catholic faith and that the Church at least permitted some arrangements whereby not all the children were raised as Catholics.

The historical argument, however, is not entirely convincing. It could be that gradually the Church has come to a clearer understanding of the divine obligation to raise all the children in the Catholic faith. Others also argue that the exceptions were merely tolerated by the Church and never approved. An evil was tolerated to avoid a greater evil. Consequently, the historical argument is open to doubts. However, if other arrangements for the education of the children were at least tolerated in the past because of particular conditions, could there not be a toleration of it today because of the existence of certain conditions?

THE PRINCIPLE OF RELIGIOUS LIBERTY

The basic arguments against the divine origin of the promise for the Catholic education of all the children stem from the principle of religious liberty and, for want of a better word, the ecumenical principle. Both of these principles have evolved only recently in the consciousness of the Church. The Second Vatican Council has approved the ecumenical principle and the declaration on religious liberty. Consequently, theologians and canonists, corresponding to the needs of our own time and the mind of the Church, must take these principles into consideration.

The position asserting the divine origin of the promises follows from the undeniable fact that the Catholic Church is the one, true Church of Christ and from the obligation of the Catholic spouse to pass on his faith to his children. No one can deny the truth of such assertions.

But perhaps there are other principles and rights involved. Despite the fact of the truth of the Catholic faith, theologians generally admit that the children of non-Catholics cannot be baptized in the Catholic faith against the wishes of their parents. According to St. Thomas, the ultimate reason is that it would be against the natural rights of the parents. Parents have a natural right and obligation to raise their children according to the dictates of their own consciences.[2]

In a mixed marriage there is a conflict of rights. Whose right predominates? If we maintain that "objective truth" can use external pressures and force against the consciences of men in good faith, we appear to deny the principle of religious liberty. Frequently in the last century the teaching of the Church has condemned religious liberty. But such condemnations arise from the false basis of religious liberty; e.g., religious indifferentism, laicism, or doctrinal relativism. According to Bishop de Smedt of Bruges in his *relatio* to the second session of the Council introducing the draft on religious liberty:

> Positively, religious liberty is the right of the human person to the free exercise of religion according to the dictates of his conscience. Negatively, it is immunity from all external force in his personal relations with God, which the conscience of man vindicates to himself. Religious liberty implies human autonomy, not from within, but certainly from without. From within man is not freed of the obligations towards the religious problem. From without, his liberty is offended when obedience to the dictates of his conscience in religious matters is impeded.[3]

Philosophically, the concept of religious liberty is based on the dignity of the human person sincerely striving to conform himself to God's will. Theologically, it is based on the truth that faith is a free gift of God to which man must freely respond.

Can we conceivably admit that a person has the right to worship God according to the dictates of his own conscience and yet deny him the right to raise his child in his own faith? Is it not a contradiction in practice? The right to educate and raise his child in his own faith is a necessary consequence of his right to worship God according to the dictates of his own conscience. Cardinal Meyer closed his address to the Council by saying, "We must give to others what we claim for ourselves."[4] It is true that in many cases non-Catholics would not be violating their conscience by raising their children in the Catholic faith. But the legislation of the Church should safeguard the right of conscience.

The freedom of conscience in religious matters is not an absolute right without any qualification. The common good and the rights of others limit the principle of religious liberty. The present paper, especially the second part, tries to show that a change in the present legislation of the Church would not be against the common good. But what about the rights of others, especially the rights of the children to be brought up in the true faith of one of their parents? From a purely juridical viewpoint (I admit it is not the best argument), the children are not yet born and are not the subjects of any rights. Faith itself is a free gift which God offers to all men; the assent of faith is free. Consequently, faith cannot be the object of any rights that man might have.

THE ECUMENICAL PRINCIPLE

The question of faith of the children takes on a different aspect in the case of mixed marriages in the strict sense. Canon 1060 says that the divine law forbids the perversion of the faith of the children. Obviously the drafters of the Code did not give attention to the principle of religious liberty as it has been accepted in the Church today. But can we even speak of a perversion of faith in mixed marriages today when some of the children are not raised Catholics? Does the raising of the child in another Christian faith put the child outside the pale of salvation? Is education and training in another Christian religion truly a perversion?

Under the influence of the ecumenical spirit the Church today recognizes the true ecclesial values in other Christian denominations. The Council Documents have referred to them as Churches.[5] We realize more today the implication of Christian baptism. Our fellow Christians do have their belief in the one Lord, one faith, and one baptism (Eph 4:5). Although they do not possess a fully developed sacramental system, they do possess him who is the primordial sacrament, Christ the Lord. Even in their liturgical assemblies, which might not be sacraments in our sense, there is a presence of Christ; the *Constitution on the Liturgy* (¶ 7) states:

> By his power he is present in the sacraments, so that when a man baptizes it is Christ himself who baptizes. He is present in his word, since it is he himself who speaks when the Holy Scriptures are read in the Church. He is present, lastly, when the Church prays and sings, for he promised: "Where two or three are gathered together in my name, there am I in the midst of them" (Matt 18:20).

It is true that children not educated in the Catholic faith would not receive the fullness of truth. But it is not the difference between night and day and all or nothing. *Per se* it would only be a question of degree.[6] The children would still be educated as Christians. The Catholic parent could also share in the Christian education of the children who would not be Catholics. We could not speak of such a Christian education as a perversion.

Some might object that the Church is never forcing the non-Catholic party to act against his conscience. A non-Catholic should not marry a Catholic if it would violate his conscience. But such an objection is not realistic. We are living in a pluralistic society where mixed marriages are a fact. Practically, the ease with which chancery offices in our country grant dispensations shows that Church authorities realize mixed marriages cannot be prevented. The Church teaches a natural law right to marriage for all men. The teaching of the Church cannot be consonant with its principles and at the same time unnecessarily restrict the natural law right to marriage. In addition, in our ecumenical age there could be a vocation from the Spirit for a particular couple to join in a mixed marriage.

What about the opinion of many theologians, and, more importantly, the statements of Benedict XIV (in his encyclical *Magnae Nobis*), Pius VIII, and Gregory XVI that it is against the natural and divine law not to bring up all the children of mixed marriages in the Catholic faith?[7] The same problem confronted those who proposed the teaching on religious liberty. Texts of Pius IX and Gregory XVI appear to deny any such principle. Bishop de Smedt in his *relatio* to the second session solved the problem by the application of the principle of progress and continuity. The documents condemned religious liberty because such teaching was based on false assumptions. The Church continues to condemn those false suppositions. But gradually the Church has come to a greater recognition of the dignity of the person and his consequent right to worship God according to the dictates of his conscience.[8] So too, the Church condemned any possibility of raising the children as non-Catholics based on false indifferentism. But today in the light of religious liberty and ecumenism there is a new and true basis for our proposed teaching.

PRACTICAL CONSIDERATIONS

What about practice? Should the Church maintain the *cautiones* for practical and disciplinary reasons? All must admit the reality: mixed marriages are a fact in our society. Theologians and canonists who are attuned to the Spirit should try to do the best they can in the present situation. I believe the Church should eliminate the *cautiones* in practice; my judgment is based on the following practical points:

1) Mixed marriages are not the ideal. The love of husband and wife demands a unity. Difficulties are bound to arise when there is disagreement over so vital a matter as religion and the education of the children. Statistics from other countries, as well as pastoral experience in our own country, point up the danger of indifferentism in mixed marriages.[9] Frequently, the children grow up with little or no religious education. For these reasons many Churches discourage mixed marriages.[10] But on the other hand, there can be and there are vocations to mixed marriages. We can never question the call of the Spirit who might be asking a particular couple to join in a mixed marriage for reasons unknown to us. In other words, we cannot flatly condemn all mixed marriages; but we must point out the difficulties they entail.

2) There is no panacea for the complex problem of mixed marriages. The difficulties connected with mixed marriages in the strict sense are symptomatic of the disunity in Christianity. We are never "going to solve the problem" of mixed marriages as long as there is a lack of unity among Christians. Legislation itself will never solve the problem. The gravest error is to assume that legislation can ever be an ultimate answer. The vital Christian faith of the spouses generally determines if the spouses and their children grow in their faith. Our primary concern is not legislation; our aim is to

strengthen the Christian faith of both partners. Mixed marriages also furnish an excellent opportunity for practical cooperation on the pastoral level with other Churches. It would be much better to work together with other Christian ministers for a good Christian home than to let the entire family slip into indifferentism and religious ignorance.

3) What would happen if the Church no longer demanded the *cautiones* in any form in the case of mixed marriages? I do not think that anyone could definitively prove that a large number of persons would be lost to the Catholic faith. It is true that some who would have been raised as Catholics under the present law would not be reared as Catholics if there were a change. But nobody dares to say that 50% of the children who under the present legislation would have been raised as Catholics would be lost to the Catholic faith if there were a change. There are many who abide by the present legislation in making the promises, but in reality they do not raise their children as Catholics. In addition, if there were no infringement on the conscience of the non-Catholic, the children would still be raised as Catholics.

Even more important is the fact that in some countries over half the mixed marriages take place outside the Catholic Church. Reliable statistics show that in the period 1950-1960 in Switzerland, 58% of all the mixed marriages were celebrated outside the Catholic Church.[11] In 1955 in Holland, 80% of the mixed marriages were not celebrated in the Catholic Church.[12] We can only speculate on the reasons behind such statistics. However, one can assume that the vast majority of the children of these mixed marriages will not be raised as Catholics. By changing its present legislation on the canonical form and the *cautiones* for mixed marriages, the Church would preserve the faith for a very large number of children and cooperate with other Churches in making the homes of mixed marriages more Christian.

One great advantage of a change in the present legislation would be the concrete evidence of the Church's belief in the principle of religious liberty. With regard to mixed marriages in the strict sense, the Church would show that it is paying more than lip service to the positive ecclesial values in Protestant Churches. The change would be a proof of our esteem and regard for other Christian Churches. The ecumenical consideration in strict mixed marriages is of the utmost importance. As true Christians we must take seriously the prayer of Christ that all may be one. Humbly we admit that our own sins have contributed to the lack of unity in Christianity. How will full unity ever be recovered? Experience seems to show that individual conversions are not the ultimate answer. In God's good plan different ecclesial traditions have been in existence for some time, and there is a positive value in other Christian traditions. The ecumenical movement aims primarily in having Christian Churches renew themselves and their own traditions. Unity will not come about by the return of some but by the growth of all.

We cannot measure what effect the change of the present laws will have on the quest for Christian unity. Like Abraham we have been called by God. We know not the exact road or the place of our destination, but in faithful response to God's call we must take the first step. Without sacrificing the truths of the faith, but in humble recognition of our own imperfections, we must strive to make the prayer of Christ a reality.

4) If the non-Catholic partner agrees, the children should be raised as Catholics. If the non-Catholic conscience would be violated by such an agreement, then the couple themselves must come to some accord. Both spouses would have to make concessions. Such a lack of agreement would be a definite source of friction in any proposed marriage.

On March 18, 1966, the Sacred Congregation for the Doctrine of the Faith issued an "Instruction on Mixed Marriages" which changes somewhat the legislation of the Code of Canon Law. Now the Ordinary can determine either in general or in individual cases if the promises should be made in writing or in another form (¶ I § 4). The instruction does mention more than once the grave duty and obligation to raise the children in the Catholic faith. "Since this obligation must be safeguarded the non-Catholic entering marriage is to be invited to promise sincerely and openly that he will in no way impede this obligation. If, however, the non-Catholic party thinks that he cannot make this promise without violating his own conscience, the Ordinary is to refer the case with all its circumstances to the Holy See" (¶ I § 3, NCWC translation).

The instruction implies that the marriage can still take place even though the non-Catholic party cannot in conscience agree to the promises. Some might argue that in this case the Church would tolerate the fact that some of the children would not be raised as Catholics. However, I do not think that one can speak of tolerating as evil the conscientious objection of the non-Catholic. Rather, the document lends support to the theory that when the conscience of the non-Catholic would be violated, there is no divine law demanding the promises. The instruction also mentions that wherever laws or customs prevent the Catholic education of the children, the Ordinary may grant the dispensation for the mixed marriage (¶ II). However, in this paragraph the document does seem to speak of tolerating the lack of religious liberty in these areas.

I hope that the new legislation is merely a step toward the elimination of the *cautiones*, as envisioned in this chapter. When the conscience of the non-Catholic would be violated there is no divine law obligation to raise all the children as Catholics, and many practical reasons call for the elimination of the *cautiones*.

Notes for Chapter 7

1.
For a complete historical evaluation of the question, see Francis J. Schenk, *Matrimonial Impediments of Mixed Religion and Disparity of Cult*, Canon Law Studies of The Catholic University of America, n. 51 (Washington, 1929). For an interpretation more favorable to the position defended in the present article, see Bernard Häring, "Mariage mixte et Concile," *Nouvelle Revue Théologique*, LXXXIV (1962), 699-708; Henry St. John, "The Problem of Mixed Marriages," *The Eastern Churches Quarterly*, XVI (1964), 155-163. For a complete bibliography on the entire subject of mixed marriages and the *cautiones*, see Ladislaus Örsy, "De forma canonica in matrimoniis mixtae religionis," *Periodica de Re Morali, Canonica, Liturgica*, LII (1963), 340-347, and "The Complex Question of Mixed Marriages," *The Heythrop Journal*, IV (1963), 385.

2.
Summa Theologiae, IIa IIae, q. 10, art. 12, in corp. See Eric D'Arcy, *Conscience and its Right to Freedom* (New York: Sheed and Ward, 1961).

3.
Emile-Joseph de Smedt, in *Council Speeches of Vatican II*, ed. H. Küng, Y. Congar, O.P., E. Hanlon, S.J. (Glen Rock: Paulist Press, 1964), p. 239. For our purposes the present essay adopts Bishop de Smedt's notion of religious liberty as a theological-moral concept. In the wider context of Church-state relations, the notion of religious liberty might better be conceived as a "juridical or constitutional concept, which has foundations in theology, ethics, political philosophy, and jurisprudence." See John Courtney Murray, "The Problem of Religious Freedom," *Theological Studies*, XXV (1964), 503-575.

4.
Quoted in a Religious News Service article by John Cogley in *The Providence Visitor*, October 2, 1964, p. 2.

5.
E.g., the *Decree on Ecumenism*, Chapter III.

6.
For a revealing discussion of the implications of the phrase, "the fullness of truth," see Charles Davis, "Unity and Christian Truth," *The Eastern Churches Quarterly*, XVI (1964), 101-116.

7.
This precise objection appeared in a letter in *The Tablet*, CCXVII (July 27, 1963), 825. For a rather complete listing of the teaching of the magisterium in the past, see Ladislaus Orsy, S.J., "Documenta Selecta de Educatione Religiosa Prolis ex Matrimonio Mixto Natae," *Periodica de Re Morali, Canonica, Liturgica*, LIII (1964), 267-284.

8.
Council Speeches of Vatican II, pp. 237-253.

9.
Francois Biot, "Mariages mixtes en Allemagne," *Istina*, VII (1960), 233- 246. Footnotes 11 and 12 contain other statistical references.

10.
E.g., James A. Pike, *If You Marry Outside Your Faith*, 2nd ed., (New York: Harper and Bros., 1962).

11.
Joseph Candolfi, "Mariages mixtes en Suisse," *Choisir*, XL (Février, 1963), 16-18.

12.
Bertulf von Leeuwen, *Het Gemengde huwelijk* (Assen: van Gorcum, 1959); "Législation des mariages mixtes et rapports entre catholiques et protestants," *Social Compass*, XI/2 (1964), 1-12.

Catholic Convictions on
Sunday Observance

Chapter Eight

Is it all right to cut the grass on Sunday? Can I go shopping at the drugstore? the supermarket? the discount house? What about ordering from Macy's on the telephone? Am I permitted to build my new house on Sunday? Is it a sin to wash, iron, and clean the house?

Such practical questions illustrate the problem of the Sunday observance. Even more baffling than the questions are the different answers priests give to the questions. There seems to be little or no agreement even among priests. Just what is forbidden on Sunday?

Canon 1248 of the Church's Code of Canon Law states:

On Sundays and other feast days of obligation Mass must be heard; moreover, there is also an obligation to abstain from servile work; from public judicial acts, and, unless lawful custom or particular permission justify them, from public marketing, the holding of fairs, and any other kind of public commercial occupation involving buying and selling.

The Code of Canon Law clearly forbids three things: servile work, public judicial or legal acts, and public business transactions. Unfortunately, the legislation does not define the meaning of the various terms. The parish priest or confessor must consult the experts to find his answer.

Not even the theologians are in agreement on the definition of servile work. The following definition is typical of many found in the theology textbooks: "The servile work here forbidden is such as is opposed to the work of a person of leisure or of an artist; e.g., plowing, sowing, tailoring. It is irrelevant that there is no reward for such work." The nature and kind of the work itself determines if it is servile.

Today many theologians wonder if such a definition remains true in our century. Two revolutions—the political revolution resulting in democratic forms of government and the industrial revolution with all its social consequences—have completely changed our way of life. There is a tendency among certain modern authors to define servile by reason of the gain or reward attached to such work. Such a definition had been proposed even before the sixteenth century. Servile work is the work done during weekdays for a salary or for the profit one hopes to make.

There is also a growing realization among theologians of the part played by the Christian people themselves in determining what is servile work. Servile work is what the average man holds to be menial and the prudent judgment and custom of instructed Christians interprets as a violation of the Sunday rest. One well known American theologian, Father

Gerald Kelly, has practically despaired of making the law workable. He tentatively suggests that it might be better to make merely an exhortation or encouragement to avoid servile work.

Confusion reigns on all sides with regard to Catholic Sunday observance. If only we had clear-cut legislation pointing out exactly what is permitted and what is forbidden. It seems that the present uncertainty is the source of all our difficulties.

But is the answer to be found in more precise laws? Is better legislation the ultimate solution? I think not. There appears to be a fallacy underlying such a solution.

THE FALLACY OF LEGALISM

The fallacy is the general impression that law and legislation make Christianity. More external laws can never be the essence of Christianity. Christianity is essentially God's love for man as manifested in creation, redemption, and the destiny of man to eternal happiness in heaven. Unfortunately, the fallacy of legalism has pervaded much of our thinking and our living. Who is a good Catholic? Everybody knows that a good Catholic is one who goes to Mass on Sunday and does not eat meat on Friday. Christ's criterion was quite different. "By this will all men know that you are my disciples if you have love for one another" (John 13:35).

Christianity is primarily love, but not external law. For example, the Church has a law about receiving Holy Communion at least once a year. This law did not exist from the beginning. When Christianity was a living, dynamic reality, there was no need to make such legislation. Only when the true spirit of Christianity declined did such a law come into existence.

Ecclesiastical legislation was never meant to be the source of Christian life. The purely ecclesiastical laws exist for the harmony of the whole Christian community and to serve the individual Christian as guide markers—to point out only the minimal demands of the Christian law of love. For the Christian who has betrayed the law of love and committed grave sin, the demands of the external law should bring him to the realization that he must seek first of all to restore his friendship and love with God. Consequently, more and better legislation cannot be the ultimate answer to the problem of the Christian observance of Sunday. Over insistence on such laws leads to the pharisaical formalism which Christ condemned so bitterly. We must seek not the letter of the law but the spirit of the law. St. Paul reminds us that "the letter kills, but the spirit gives life" (2 Cor 3:6).

THE SPIRIT OF THE LAW

What is the real meaning, the spirit of the law of Sunday rest? Here another fallacy exists. Many people believe that Sunday rest is merely a continuation of the Sabbath observance in the old law. The very use of the word servile work, a Sabbatarian term, gives credence to such an identification. Scripture tells us that in the time of Christ the observance of the Sabbath was formal and legalistic. The idea of rest became the be-all and the end-all—something sacred in itself. Sabbath observance was a dismal, unappealing, and repressive blue-law affair. Such a blue-law Sabbatical observance has its Christian counterpart in the Calvinist Sunday of Scotland or the Puritan Sunday of New England. Such a concept of Sunday is repelling and even non-Christian. It is no wonder that people had to be forced to observe it through minute laws and regulations!

Today we are becoming increasingly aware of the obligation to give free exercise of conscience to those who observe another day in the week and not Sunday. Many voices fear that as a result of a relaxation in our civil laws the whole Christian concept of Sunday will be destroyed.

Such fears appear to be rooted in the twofold fallacy mentioned above. A legalistic mentality puts too much emphasis on legislation as the primary way to bring about a Christian observance of Sunday. Likewise, such anxiety over Sabbatarian laws tends to equate the Christian Sunday and a blue-law observance. True Sunday observance will be a reality only to the extent that we Christians understand and put into practice the true spirit of Sunday and its rest. Hence the pressing need to know the true meaning of Sunday.

HISTORICAL INVESTIGATION

An historical and theological consideration of the meaning of the Lord's Day and the Sunday rest will give a true insight into the nature, purpose, and obligations of the Sunday observance. Such a consideration must avoid one very possible pitfall. We cannot and do not want to turn back the clock. There is no sense in lamenting the "good old days." From the lessons of history, however, we can see better what must be done in twentieth century America. This is an authentic Christian approach—a practical extension of the fundamental Christian doctrine of the incarnation. Just as Christ was present to the people of his day as one of them, so we must make Christianity and Christ present in the existential conditions of contemporary American life and civilization.

The writings of the early Fathers of the Church show us the real meaning of the Christian Sunday. It is not a continuation of the Sabbath in the sense of setting aside a day of rest. The Lord's Day with its Sunday rest came into existence independently of the Jewish Sabbath and the third commandment of the decalogue given to Moses on Mt. Sinai. The basic idea of Sunday is the day of the resurrection—hence a day of joy, triumph, peace, and hope.

The very name, the Lord's Day (*Dies Dominica*), shows the connection with the resurrection. Christ becomes the Lord through his resurrection, which in the early Church was the crowning point of the redemption. Christ triumphed over sin and death and was exalted by the Father, who made him the Lord. From heaven the resurrected Lord and the Father send the Spirit to men so they can share in the victory and joy of the resurrection. The name which is above every name is the name of Christ, the Lord.

Sunday is par excellence the day of participation in the resurrection, the salvific paschal mystery. The creation of light in the beginning of the world prefigures Sunday. Sunday is the first day of the new creation when the light of salvation overcomes the darkness of sin. Since Sunday symbolizes the completion of creation through redemption, the Fathers frequently refer to it as the eighth day. Also, the effects of the salvific paschal mystery of the resurrection belong to Sunday. The sending of the Spirit by the resurrected Lord occurs on Easter Sunday. The more solemn sending of the Holy Spirit takes place on Pentecost Sunday.

The center of this Christ-orientated day was naturally the Eucharistic banquet, which renews the paschal mystery and puts Christians into direct contact with the resurrected Lord. Fasting was forbidden on Sunday because of its joyful character. At Mass, the Christians did not kneel. By standing, they expressed their joy and their preparedness for the final coming of Christ. Their Sunday joy and triumph made them look forward with hope to the full consummation of that joy and peace in heaven. Briefly, this is the meaning of Sunday in the early Church—the day of the resurrection, of triumph, of peace, of joy—the day of worship dedicated to the risen Lord and centered on the Eucharistic banquet.

THE NEW LAW FULFILLS THE OLD LAW

The Old Testament Sabbath was essentially a day of rest in remembrance of creation and the covenant. In this manner, the devout Jew gave worship to God. The Jewish law forbade all work on the Sabbath, whereas on feast days the law prohibited just servile work. In practice, however, the Jewish Sabbath became formalistic and legalistic, a seemingly senseless burden placed on man.

Sunday completely replaced the Sabbath. The Sabbath with all its legal formalities was no longer binding for the Christian. However, in the whole context of salvation history and God's relationship with man, the old covenant prefigures the new covenant. In the words of Christ, the new law fulfills the old law. Guided by such a principle, the Fathers of the Church initiated a comparison between Sunday and the Sabbath. But the primitive Church did not compare the Sabbath rest with the Sunday rest. The early Fathers gave a spiritual meaning and interpretation to the Sabbath rest. Sunday fulfills the purpose of the Sabbath by making the Christian share in the peace and rest of the resurrected Lord. The Christian thus looks forward eagerly to the eternal peace of heaven which the Old Testament law signified in a very imperfect manner. The Fathers interpret the Old Testament prohibition of feast day servile work as a prohibition of sinful actions on Sunday. Sin is the servile work of the Christian. Sin enslaves man and takes away from him his Christian freedom. The Fathers of the Church urge the Christian to avoid such slavery on all days but especially on Sunday.

ORIGIN OF THE CHRISTIAN LAW OF SUNDAY REST

How then did the law of Sunday rest develop in the Church? In the time of the Apostolic Fathers and the early

Christian period, there is no evidence of a prohibition of work on Sunday. Tertullian (+220?) is the first to mention the Sunday rest. For him it is not a law but a necessary consequence of an authentic Christian disposition. The Sunday rest is a bodily sharing in the joy of the resurrection and affords the Christian the opportunity to worship God, especially at the Eucharistic banquet. The first legislation about Sunday rest was a civil law of the Emperor Constantine in 321. The law itself stems from pagan Roman law about feast days and not from Jewish Sabbatarian law. For example, the law did not forbid working in the fields. Note well the purpose of the first law of Sunday rest—to enable the Christians to participate in the Eucharistic sacrifice.

Even up to the sixth century there is evidence against the existence of an ecclesiastical law of Sunday rest. A sermon attributed to Eusebius of Alexandria (probably dating from the sixth century) does speak of Sunday rest as a grave command of divine origin and does introduce Sabbatarian and sociological motivation for it. Caesarius of Arles (+542) introduced the "all the more" argument: if the Jews abstained from all work on the Sabbath, all the more Christians should abstain from work on the Lord's Day. Martin of Braga (+580) was the first person to make the step from Sabbatarian comparison to Sabbatarian terminology with regard to the Sunday rest. He introduced the term servile work to denote the work a Christian should avoid on Sunday. Martin, however, reflected the common teaching in showing that the prohibition of servile work stemmed from the nature of the Lord's Day and not the Sabbath.

The century immediately before Charlemagne saw the vitality of Christianity at a low ebb. With regard to Sunday rest, the penal and juridic aspects of the law suffocated the spirit of the Sunday rest. The Old Testament formula introduced by Martin of Braga prepared the way for Old Testament motivation of the Sunday rest. The Carolingian reform brought back the true spirit of the law, but Sabbatarian terminology and motivation also remained.

Gradually the prohibition of work on Sunday had made its way into both civil and ecclesiastical laws. The Decree of Gratian (1140), a private compilation of existing Church legislation, mentions the prohibition of work, but not the term servile work. The Decretals of Gregory IX, an authentic and official collection of the laws of the Church, does refer to prohibited servile works. Henceforth, the term servile work becomes a permanent part of the ecclesiastical legislation on Sunday rest.

THE SCHOLASTIC SYNTHESIS

The great Catholic theologians of the scholastic period (thirteenth century) developed a systematic theology of the Sunday rest. Earlier in the Church's history there was neither the maturity nor the theological leisure necessary to construct a systematic theology of the Sunday rest. Briefly, the scholastics accepted the Old Testament terminology of servile work; but the prohibition of servile work did not exist merely for the sake of rest. The prohibition of work is subordinate to and flows from the nature of Sunday as the day of the worship of the resurrected Lord. The Sabbath law of the Old Testament was merely ceremonial and does not oblige Christians. The natural law does demand that man give worship to God. Since man must occupy himself with the problem of daily living, he cannot dedicate himself entirely to the actual worship of God. Consequently, man sets aside certain days and places for the worship of God. Such is the divine and natural foundation of an ecclesiastical law of Sunday rest established not by God but by the Church.

The scholastic theologians unanimously adopted the term servile work for the work forbidden on Sunday. In a spiritual and primary sense, sin is servile work. In a material sense, servile work is that which prevents man from freely serving God in the same way that slaves cannot freely give themselves to the service of another master. Sunday is a day of worship of God by the whole Christian community. Whatever disturbs such communal public worship is against the Sunday rest. Since Sunday rest is only a Church law, the scholastics admit necessity, piety, and custom as reasons which excuse from the observance of the law.

A LEGALISTIC ATTITUDE REASSERTS ITSELF

After the time of St. Thomas and scholasticism there was a disintegration of theology. Departmentalization set in and the influence of the positive science of canon law became prominent in moral theology. After the Council of Trent (sixteenth century), moral theology became orientated toward training the priest as a confessor to judge the gravity of sins. The question of what constitutes a sin against the law of Sunday rest preoccupied the theologians. Unfortunately the theologians no longer considered the law of Sunday rest in its proper context. The concept of Sunday rest was seen only in relation to the law and not to the very meaning and essence of the Lord's Day. Despite the overemphasis on the legalistic aspect of Sunday rest, the different definitions mentioned earlier show that even today there is no agreement on what precisely constitutes servile work.

CONCLUSIONS REGARDING SUNDAY REST

The theological and historical investigation just made shows that the Sunday rest derives its meaning and its very existence not from Church law but from the significance of the Lord's Day. God, not man, made Sunday. The spirit of God and not human legislation must pervade the entire observance of Sunday. The Church law performs only a secondary function; that is, to point out what are the minimal demands of Sunday rest. Although secondary, positive law cannot be neglected. However, we are suffering from the opposite error, for the purely legal aspect of Sunday rest has been overstressed.

The Sunday rest exists primarily for worship. Sunday is the day of the Lord who has given us the most precious gift of all —his love, our sanctification. Man's answer to God's gift is the gift of himself, his worship. "What shall I return to the Lord for all that he has given to me?" (Psalm 115). The union of God sanctifying and man worshiping culminates in man's full participation in the Eucharistic banquet. The Mass is the most perfect form of worship. Not just the individual, but all men saved by the paschal mystery of Christ should gather together around the banquet table of the Lord. The primary function of the Sunday rest is to allow time for participating in the worship of the Mass and carrying out the spirit of worship throughout the day.

Christians must understand and live the Sunday rest in its essential relation with the day which the Lord has made. The prohibition of servile work has a value and purpose only in connection with the meaning of Sunday. The Lord's Day, the day of the resurrection, is a day of joy, triumph, and peace. On Sunday the body should share in the joy of the soul. Christian theology has always taught the close inter-relationship between the body and the soul. On Sunday the whole man should share in the victory of Christ over sin. Original sin condemned man to work by the sweat of his brow. Sharing in Christ's triumph, man should free himself from the bonds of such labor.

Likewise, in a special way on Sunday the Christian should share in the peace of the Lord's Day. Christ's first words to the Apostles on the night of his resurrection were: "Peace be to you." Modern man has no peace. His ceaseless external activity is symbolic of his restless spirit. Man throws himself into his work and just as rambunctiously throws himself into his recreation in an attempt to "get away from it all." Modern man is restless; he is always running away from something; he has no peace. He lacks the peace of the resurrection and the freedom of the sons of God. The joy, triumph, and peace of the Christian Sunday are a sign and at the same time a pledge of the eternal joy, eternal triumph, and eternal peace of heaven.

FROM THEORY TO PRACTICE

The question of Sunday observance well illustrates the secondary place of law in the life of the Church. If the fervor of the Christian people had continued there would have been no need for a law. The letter of the law always assumes a greater importance whenever the life of the Church is at low ebb. Law itself is also incapable of bringing about any renewal. Renewal does not come from legislation; in fact, an accentuation on law hampers renewal. If all the emphasis is placed on the law and its obligation, the Church almost forgets to look at the reality itself. For example, moral theology textbooks devote many pages to the grave obligation of clerics in major orders to recite the Latin, monastic breviary. Only recently has the Church come to the realization that such a breviary might not be the best form of prayer for a priest in the active ministry. With its tendency to institutionalize and make permanent, law frequently hampers change and renewal. Worse yet, the Church often begins to imitate civil societies by putting primary reliance on the coercive force and sanctions of law to bring about "a better Christian life." Is it really a serious matter to miss one small hour of the breviary or even the whole breviary prayer for one day? An over-emphasis on law and its sanctions robs the Church of its very life—the loving power of the Spirit. Law can play a pedagogical and educational role in the Church, but only insofar as it reflects the living Spirit.

How can we make Sunday observance a living reality in our lives? Legislation is not the ultimate answer to the problem of Sunday rest. Nor can any theologian tell the Christian people precisely how Sunday should be observed. A theologian can and should reveal the true meaning of the Sunday rest. But it is only through a dialogue among all the members of the Church that we can work out in practice the proper Christian observance of Sunday. It is against the dignity and the obligations of the layman for him to expect the theologian to give a pat answer to the question. The layman and the theologian, together with the hierarchy, must cooperate in such a venture. All of us together, the people of God on earth, can bring about a true renewal of the meaning of Sunday. We must first incorporate it into our own lives and family circles. The best way to teach Sunday observance to others is not by legislation but by the witness and testimony of real Christian people.

In an address in 1947 to the men of Catholic Action in Italy, Pope Pius XII summarized the challenge that is ours today: "Sunday must become again the day of the Lord, the day of adoration, of glorification of God, of the Holy Sacrifice, of prayers, of rest, of recollection and reflection; the day of happy reunion in the intimate circle of the family. . . . Here a vast field of activity awaits you. Go forth courageously to the work, and help to give Sunday back to God, to Christ, to the Church, to peace, and to the happiness of families."

The Relevance of
Moral Theology Today

Chapter Nine

In general, relevance in theology means that the Word of God is presented in a meaningful way to contemporary man. For moral theology today, I see four particular areas of relevance: the biblical, the liturgical, the contemporary, and the philosophical. This chapter will merely discuss some of the problems and questions facing contemporary moral theology in these areas.

BIBLICAL

The most devastating charge leveled against moral theology maintains that many presentations of morality do not appear to be particularly Christian. The reason is obvious: moral theology has not found its basic orientation and inspiration in the Word of God itself. The structure of the manuals of moral theology follows the system of the theological and moral virtues or the ten commandments, neither of which is characteristically Christian. A biblically orientated moral theology (and there can be no other theology worthy of the name Christian) shows that Christian morality stems from the new heart which God has given to his people. In response to the loving gift of God, man's whole life becomes the gift of himself to God and neighbor.

Likewise, the particular questions treated in moral theology sometime pass over the teaching of scripture on the subject. For example, how often in connection with the sacrament of penance and the forgiveness of sins do theologians or catechists or preachers mention that our sins will be forgiven only to the extent that we are willing to forgive our enemies? Yet every day we pray in the Our Father: "Forgive us our trespasses as we forgive those who trespass against us." Luke includes among the rules of charity: "Forgive, and you shall be forgiven" (Luke 6:37). The parable of the unmerciful servant reminds Christians that we must forgive our enemies just as our heavenly Father has forgiven us (Mark 18:21-35). How much space in the manuals of moral theology is given to the love of enemies? But love of enemies is the unique characteristic of Christian morality. Even the gentiles and pagans love their friends. Love becomes easy when we are loved in return, but true Christian love does not need reciprocity. Christian love reflects the love of the Father whose sun shines on the just and the unjust and the love of the Son who gave himself for all men without any thought of a return (Matt 5:43-47; Luke 6:27-38).

But a closer examination of the moral demands of the New Testament reveals a perplexing problem of relevancy. The Sermon on the Mount, the description of charity in John and Paul, the complete openness to God and neighbor expressed throughout the New Testament are sublime and beautiful. But are they practical, relevant, and meaningful for our modern world? Read through the Sermon on the Mount. Forgive seventy times seven—Do not worry about what you shall eat or drink—Turn the other cheek—Give to everyone who asks—Do not invite your rich acquaintances to your party. Yes, the ethical precepts of Christ are beautiful and sublime; but they seem completely irrelevant and impractical in our everyday life situation.

How can we solve the problem?[1] Perhaps moralists in the past have been right in ignoring the moral conduct outlined by Christ. Maybe we should in an embarrassed way sweep New Testament morality under the rug and try to forget about it. Some Christian scholars have tried to explain away the ethic proposed by Christ as a form of oriental exaggeration. Some believe that Christ is talking about the final state of the kingdom and describing conduct in the future and not in the present. Others think that Christ is proposing an interim ethic, a very severe and intense period of preparation before the final coming which will occur very soon. Or perhaps the demands of Christ are directed merely to a chosen few and not to all. A true Christian, however, must take seriously the ethical demands of Christ. But how are they relevant?

The ethical directives of Christ are relevant because they bring man to the realization of the primary and fundamental truth of the Christian life—it is God who saves. The Christian who meditates on the radical and absolute ethical demands of the gospel can never say: "All these things I have kept from my youth." The Christian conscience attuned to the ethical demands of Christ comes to the realization of the truth of the first beatitude, the cornerstone of the Christian life: "How blest are those who know that they are poor; the Kingdom of heaven is theirs."[2] My inability to observe the New

Testament ethics reminds me that salvation is God's gift.

Unfortunately, our practice frequently fails to mirror the primary truth of Christianity. The ordinary Catholic in the street would say he is saved by observing the commandments. Christianity often becomes a set of static laws that are capable of being fulfilled to the letter. The man who lives up to these laws naturally takes a sense of pride in his accomplishments. Christ's condemnation of the Pharisees applies in a very poignant way to some Christians today: "Woe to you, Scribes and Pharisees, hypocrites! because you pay tithes on mint and anise and cummin, and have left undone the weightier matters of the Law, right judgment and mercy and faith" (Matt 23:23; See Luke 11:42). A chorus of voices is condemning legalism today, and rightly so; but underlying legalism is the pelagian mentality that man saves himself by doing the works of the law.

But the ethical teaching of Christ must do more than bring man to a recognition of his own weakness and the saving power of God.[3] Man cooperates with the gift of God. The Christian conduct outlined by Christ has a place in the life of the sincere Christian living in the modern world. How can the Christian take seriously the seemingly impossible and impractical ethics of Christ? The moral demands of the gospel indicate the goal and direction of all true Christian conduct. The Christian continually strives to incorporate more and more of the divine agape into his daily actions. The Christian tends in a real way to give himself completely and without reserve to the call of the kingdom. Growth and continual conversion mark the life of the Christian who seeks to share more fully in the disinterested love of God.[4] The Vatican Council reminds us that the Church is in pilgrimage, but each Christian is also a pilgrim travelling ever closer to his goal of perfect union with God and neighbor.

Today some theologians are stressing the idea of compromise; i.e., in the human condition man frequently has to compromise with the absolute ethical sayings of the New Testament.[5] Situations arise where certain values must be sacrificed either partially or totally for the sake of higher values. In fact, no human act is ever perfectly good. Rather than a theology of compromise, a theology of growth and continual conversion would give a more positive meaning to the same reality.

Many problems about the particular ethical sayings of Christ remain. In general, however, the radical demands of the New Testament ethic are relevant in a twofold manner: (1) The absolute character of the New Testament ethics reminds us that we are saved by God and not by ourselves. (2) Man, nevertheless, must continually strive to obtain the goal of complete openness in a union of love with God and neighbor.

LITURGICAL

Both the Old and the New Testament remind us that morality springs from man's relationship with the saving person of God and not with a code or law. Christian morality is the living out of the Christian life we have received. Joachim Jeremias refers to the Christian life as "lived faith."[6] As the scholastic axiom expresses the reality: *agere sequitur esse.* According to St. Paul, "If we live by the Spirit, by the Spirit let us also walk" (Gal 5:25). The Christian life, like the good tree, brings forth good fruit, the fruits of the Spirit. In other words the Christian life is merely—doing what comes supernaturally. The liturgy becomes the great source and school of Christian morality, for in the liturgy the Christian receives and grows in the life-giving love of God. Through their liturgical life Christians become conscious of their being and their destiny.

Another characteristic of Christian morality is its dialogical structure, man's loving response to the gift of God. The liturgy above all else emphasizes the Christian life as the response of man to the call of God. The Word and work of God in the liturgy invite the Christian to respond and to become in his daily life the vigilant servant, watching and waiting to hear the call of God. People ask: "How are we going to teach the new emphases in morality?" The answer: the liturgy must become the great school of the Christian life.

Morality has no connection with the liturgy for those who conceive morality in terms of obedience to laws. Such a misunderstanding of moral theology is still widespread. The Church is most thankful for the enlightened *Constitution on the Sacred Liturgy;* but even the framers of such an advanced document do not properly understand the nature of moral theology. Paragraph 16 reminds seminary professors: "Moreover, other professors, while striving to expound the mystery of Christ and the history of salvation from the angle proper to each of their own subjects, must nevertheless do so in a way which will clearly bring out the connection between their subjects and the liturgy, as also the unity which underlies all priestly training. This consideration is especially important for professors of dogmatic, spiritual, and pastoral theology and for those of scripture." No mention is made of moral theology. And yet moral theology above all considers the living of "the mystery of Christ and the history of salvation."

CONTEMPORARY

The scriptures describe the life of agape, but theology must show the reality of agape in the daily life of the modern Christian. Theology must put flesh and blood on the command of Christ: "You therefore are to be perfect, even as your heavenly Father is perfect" (Matt 6:48). Especially in the light of the fifth chapter of the constitution on the Church, "The Universal Vocation to Holiness in the Church," moral theology needs to spell out the meaning of Christianity in our day. All realize that man's response to the reign of God consists in the wholehearted giving of self to God and neighbor. But even the seemingly ordinary human actions, the humdrum day to day activities, serve for building up the new heaven and the new earth. Contemporary thought needs to develop better a theology of the meaning of the world, earthly realities, work, technology, culture, art, leisure, etc. However, theology should not succumb to the temptation of building a new legalism in place of the old. Perhaps moral theology should discuss with examples how the Christian works for the coming kingdom of God in his home, his work, and his recreation. For example, in courses on marriage the students could discuss the application of the Sermon on the Mount to the daily life of husband and wife—how a married couple needs to communicate with one another and to share their joys and sorrows, be it washing dishes, shining shoes, changing diapers or celebrating birthdays.

Modern moral theology will fulfill its purpose only if it employs the findings of modern science especially in the fields of sociology, anthropology and psychology. For example, considerations of sin should center on the idea of breaking a personal relationship with God and not stress sin as the breaking of a law or a blot on the soul. The whole question of the emotions and the unconscious enters into the consideration of man's loving response to God.

PHILOSOPHICAL

Theology, in its effort to make the Word of God meaningful for contemporary man, employs some philosophical understanding of man and the world. Catholic moral theology generally bases its consideration of human actions on the natural law philosophy. Catholic theology, to its great credit, has always tried to uphold the dignity, grandeur, and meaningfulness of all that is natural and human. The acclaim accorded *Pacem in Terris* shows that within a natural law framework the Church can speak in a relevant way to the modern world. But today theologians and philosophers are calling for a rethinking of the natural law. Catholic thinkers are raising questions both with regard to the morality of particular human actions and the whole general theory of natural law.

Many are raising questions about the morality of particular human actions. The birth control controversy has forced moral theologians to critically examine the consideration of the moral goodness or badness of a human action. Perhaps the most succinct statement of the problem is: What constitutes the human moral act—the material substratum alone, the intention alone, or both in some combination?[7]

The classical example frequently mentioned is the transplantation of organs. Theologians traditionally maintained that mutilation of an organ was morally justifiable for the good of the individual or for punitive reasons. Then the question of transplantation arose. Some theologians condemned the transplantation of organs because a mutilation could be morally justified only if it were done for the good of the individual or for punitive reasons. But today most theologians allow transplantation as an act of charity and love of neighbor. Excising an organ is really not a mutilation if the organ is given to another person. The human act involved is not the mere material act of mutilation, but the total human act is transplantation. Even though the material substratum of the act involves excising an organ, such an act is not a human act of mutilation but the human act of transplantation.[8] Theology cannot identify the material substratum with the human act.

W. Van Der Marck extends the same type of reasoning to the anovulatory pills. (Logically, the same reasoning seems to extend to all forms of contraception.) The use of the pill according to theologians can be either therapeutic or contraceptive. But what about a third possibility? What about using the pill for fertility control? The mere taking of the pill is not a human act—the purpose must somehow enter into the human act.[9]

There are other questions where theologians seem to be probing to find an answer to the more general question of what constitutes a human act. One moralist maintains that masturbation for seminal analysis is not morally wrong. Just a human consideration, now buttressed by modern psychology, indicates that such an act is not the human act of masturbation. Even though the act has the same material substratum as masturbation, the human act in this case is an act of obtaining semen for analysis.[10] Another example: the soldier who kills himself lest he betray secrets to the enemy. The material act is suicide, but the human act is not suicide but the protection of one's country. A more striking example: "An act may or may not be abortion as a human act although materially and externally it is nevertheless exactly the same act. If doctors decide that the removal of a fetus is medically necessary, and if this is humanly acceptable, then it is not abortion (except perhaps in purely medical or physiological terms), and the principle that abortion is murder still applies."[11]

But immediately the objection comes to mind: all these examples violate the axiom that the end does not justify the means. However, in all the cases mentioned the means does not seem to be a truly human act. It is not the human act of mutilation or masturbation or abortion or suicide. The axiom about the end not justifying the means does not seem to apply when the means is not a human act. The same material substratum, e.g., excising a kidney, could be a therapeutic act or a mutilation or a transplantation.[12]

Responsible philosophers and theologians are now questioning and trying to rethink the whole concept of natural law. The natural law or unwritten law is "an order or dispensation which human reason can discover and according to which the human will must act to attune itself to the necessary ends of the human being."[13] Our being is a dynamic totality which is constantly trying to achieve and fulfill itself. The natural law demands that all the particular dynamisms and tendencies of man be in accord with his fundamental dynamic structure, his nature. The natural law theory is founded on the teleology of the individual substance which strives to fully achieve itself. Natural law theoreticians object to the "false idea of natural law . . . drawn from the pages of cheapjack textbooks."[14] The natural law properly understood is not legalistic, over-rationalistic, biological, abstract or immobile.[15]

However, some scholars are still not satisfied.[16] The glory of the natural law theory, at least in my opinion, is its correspondence to reality—the ontological basis of man's actions. Right and wrong correspond to being and not to mere whim or fancy. But perhaps the concept of being heretofore generally accepted among natural law thinkers does not correspond to reality as we know it today. Yes, morality is grounded in being; but being is perhaps more personal, more historical, and more relational than the concept of being in traditional natural law theory.

The natural law theory stresses the natural, whereas modern thought puts most emphasis on the personal. Is not the person something more than just an individuated nature? Moral considerations must begin with the human person and his relations with other persons, especially The Other.[17] As a practical application, it would seem that the principle of totality with regard to the human person should also include the generative and reproductive organs when the functioning of such organs becomes proportionately harmful to the person.

To overcome the static and immutable characteristics of many natural law interpretations, scholars today mention the historicity of the natural law. The historical element adds another dimension to our concept of reality. Historical circumstances modify reality and morality.[18] Situation and time play a vital role in our ordinary life. Ecclesiastes (3:1) reminds us: "There is an appointed time for everything, and a time for every affair under the heavens." Timing is a most important factor in human action, be it taking out an insurance policy, asking the boss for a raise, or entering a political race. Consequently, developments can occur which make something right today which was not always right in a different situation.

The relational character of reality stands out today. Can philosophy merely consider the human person as a *subsistens distinctum* completely separated from all reality? Rather, it appears that the individual in many cases is what he is precisely because of his relationships with others. Emphasis on relations is not foreign to Catholic thought, for the persons of the Trinity are constituted as subsistent relations. Is it a true picture of reality to consider a particular nature as completely constituted in itself and isolated from all other reality?[19] Philosophy must consider the relatedness of a particular being with all other beings and with the fullness of being.[20] As already stated in more personalist terms, man exists primarily in his relationships with others, especially The Other.

Another recasting of natural law theory revolves around the theory of values. The natural law underscores the importance of certain human and natural values. However, such values do not exist as absolutely independent in themselves, but they must be in harmony with other values. Likewise an evolving human consciousness can come to a greater appreciation of particular values; e.g., the dignity and freedom of the human person. External norms will change and develop because of the changing and developing relationships among the many different human values. The external norms or laws have a meaning only insofar as they express and protect definite human values.[21]

But why all the rethinking today? Why the dissatisfaction with the explanation of the natural law as it appears in philosophy and theology manuals? From the point of view of an ethician, the questioning stems from the tension that is apparent between the absolute character of formal principles and the very complex reality of modern life. The formal principle, e.g., thou shalt not kill, has no material content as such. The principle cannot apply absolutely to all reality. In the developing course of history, Catholic thought has come to grips with the problem through various means: the theory of direct and indirect killing, the concept of killing in self-defense, the just war theory. St. Thomas experienced the same tension, for he declares that the conclusions or practical applications of the common principles of the natural law are true only in the majority of cases.[22] The highly complex technological and scientific world in which we live, together with our historical knowledge, merely accentuates the tension between absolute norms and concrete reality. The very make-up of our life and society demands that we should be even more aware of the problem than the perceptive thirteenth century theologian.[23]

The objection quickly comes to mind. All such considerations lead to situation ethics and open the door to pure subjectivism.[24] Perhaps not. To avoid subjectivism morality must be based on being. Perhaps being is more personal, historical, and relational than the concept of being underlying some presentations of the natural law.

All must agree that morality cannot be reduced merely to good intentions. Actions also count. Love and truth must go hand in hand. Our own daily experience testifies to the insufficiency of intentions. The fact that a person has a "big heart" does not excuse the stupidity of his actions. From a theological point of view, actions are important, for man is cooperating with God in the work of bringing about the new heaven and the new earth. But a theory that gives more prominence to values or to the personal, relational or historical aspect of being does not necessarily lead to subjectivism and relativism in the bad sense. Take as an example the relationship between a parent and child. The love and protection of the parent will always be present, but the parent's love will express itself in different ways. A parent will tell a three year old child never to cross the street. As the child grows older, the parent teaches him how to cross the street safely. I am trying to show that external norms can change with changing relationships, but changing norms do not always imply a false subjectivism. Much work, however, remains to be done in the philosophical understanding which moral theology must employ in its consideration of man and the world.

The present chapter raises many questions and attempts few answers.[25] The purpose has been to show the direction that moral theology needs to follow in the attempt to be relevant in our contemporary world. Above all else moral theology can never forget its primary function—to bring mankind and the whole world into an ever greater participation in the life and love of God.

Notes for Chapter 8

1.

Unfortunately, Catholic moralists seem to have given little or no attention to the question of the relevancy of the ethics of the New Testament. For a very detailed and analytic study of the general theme of the ethics of the New Testament which is especially valuable for the ample bibliography, see C. Spicq, O.P., *Théologie Morale du Nouveau Testament*, 2 vols. (Paris: J. Gabalda, 1965). Among Protestant scripture scholars who have considered the question of the relevancy of the ethics of Christ, see John Knox, *The Ethic of Jesus in the Teaching of the Church* (New York: Abingdon Press, 1961); also, C. H. Dodd, *Gospel and Law* (Cambridge, England: Cambridge University Press, 1950).

2.

Matt 5:3. The translation taken from the *New English Bible* is quoted in an approving way by C. Spicq, Vol. II, p. 755.

3.

The failure to consider the cooperation of man appears in some Protestant interpretations of Christian ethical conduct and also in the so-called "mystique of sin." See Louis Monden, S.J., *Sin, Liberty and Law* (New York: Sheed and Ward, 1965), pp. 145-166.

4.

Bernard Häring, C.SS.R., "La conversion," in *Pastorale du péché*, ed. Ph. Delhaye (Tournai: Desclee, 1961), pp. 65-145.

5.

A. J. van Ouwerkerk, C.SS.R., "Gospel Morality and Human Compromise," in *Moral Problems and Christian Personalism*, Vol. V of *Concilium* (New York: Paulist Press, 1965), pp. 7-21.

6.

Joachim Jeremias, *The Sermon on the Mount* (Philadelphia: Fortress Press, 1963), p. 34.

7.
For a speculative consideration of the relationship between object and end in the theology of St. Thomas, see S. Pinckaers, O.P. "Le rôle de la fin dans l'action morale selon saint Thomas," in *Le Renouveau de la morale* (Paris: Casterman, 1964), pp. 114-143.

8.
W. Van der Marck, O.P., "Vruchtbaarheidsregeling: poging tot antwoord op een nog open vraag," *Tijdschrift voor Theologie*, III (1963), pp. 378-413. An English summary is found on p. 413.

9.
Van der Marck, English summary, p. 413.

10.
Bernard Häring, C.SS.R. proposed such an opinion as probable during a two week course for professors and others interested in moral theology at Regis College, Toronto, Canada, July, 1963.

11.
W. Van der Marck, O.P., *Love and Fertility* (London: Sheed and Ward, 1965), pp. 59-60.

12.
For a recent critique on the distinction between direct and indirect, see P. Knauer, S.J., "La détermination du bien et du mal morale par le principe du double effet," *Nouvelle Revue Théologique*, 87 (1965), pp. 356-376; especially note the critique and ample bibliography given by Van der Marck, *Love and Fertility*, pp. 35-63.

13.
Jacques Maritain, *The Rights of Man and Natural Law* (New York: Charles Scribner's Sons, 1943), p. 61.

14.
Maritain, p. 59.

15.
E. G., John Courtney Murray, S.J., "The Doctrine Lives:

The Eternal Return of Natural Law," in *We Hold These Truths* (New York: Sheed and Ward, 1960), pp. 295-336.

16.
Valuable summaries of present day thinking about natural law include: *Moral Problems and Christian Personalism*, Vol. V. of *Concilium* (New York: Paulist Press, 1965); *Light on the Natural Law*, ed. Illtud Evans, O.P. (London: Burns and Oates, 1965).

17.
"In the consideration of man it requires the clear primacy of actual personal existence over essential, natured individuality. In ethics it requires the relocation and subordination of the natural law."—Cited from the galley proofs of an address by Kenneth Schmitz to the annual convention of the Society of Catholic College Teachers of Sacred Doctrine, St. Louis, April 19, 1965. The address will be published in the *Proceedings*. The same emphasis on the personal, seen especially from the psychological point of view, appears in Marc Oraison, *Une morale pour notre temps* (Paris: Fayard, 1964); and in an even more radical way in Ignace Lepp, *The Authentic Morality* (New York: Macmillan, 1965).

18.
Josef Fuchs, S.J., *Natural Law: A Theological Investigation* (New York: Sheed and Ward, 1965), especially Chapter V and VI. However, it does not seem that Fuchs' treatment would satisfy the authors mentioned in footnotes 16 and 17.

19.
Robert O. Johann, S.J. has expressed such ideas in papers read at the annual meetings of the American Society for Christian Ethics, Washington, D.C., January 21-23, 1965, and the Catholic Theological Society of America, Denver, June 21-24, 1965. The latter paper will be published in the *Proceedings*.

20.
The terms "relatedness" or "relational" avoid the pejorative connotations of "relative." The above suggestion, to my

knowledge, was first proposed by Paul Ramsey, "The Transformation of Ethics," in *Faith and Ethics: The Theology of H. Richard Niebuhr*, ed. Paul Ramsey (New York: Harper and Row, 1957), p. 142. The same essay was later reprinted in Paul Ramsey, *Nine Modern Moralists* (Englewood Cliffs: Prentice-Hall, 1962), pp. 149, 179.

21.
Such a theory seems to be the conclusion of the historical study of natural law and contraception by John T. Noonan, Jr., *Contraception* (Cambridge: Harvard University Press, 1965), p. 533.

22.
Ia IIae, q. 94, art. 4, "Sed ratio practica negotiatur circa contingentia, in quibus sunt operationes humanae: et ideo, etsi in communibus sit aliqua necessitas, quanto magis ad propria descenditur, tanto magis invenitur defectus. . . . Sed quantum ad quaedam propria, quae sunt quasi conclusiones principiorum communium, est eadem apud omnes ut in pluribus et secundum rectitudinem et secundum notitiam."

23.
Protestant ethical thought has generally seen in the tension between formal principles and concrete reality the starting point for two different types of ethical systems—an ethics of principles and a contextual ethics. A recent survey reveals that even contextualists see the need for some type of principles—George H. Easter, "New Frontiers in Protestant Contextual Ethics," an unpublished address delivered at the annual meeting of the American Society for Christian Ethics, Washington, January 22, 1965. For an interesting attempt to avoid the complete dichotomy between principles and context, see James M. Gustafson, "Context versus Principles: A Misplaced Debate in Christian Ethics," *Harvard Theological Review*, 58 (1965), pp. 171-202.

24.
For a consideration of situation ethics from the Catholic

point of view which generally follows the moderate thinking of Karl Rahner, S.J., see J. Goffinet, *Morale de situation et morale chrétienne* (Bruxelles: La Pensée Catholique, 1963) . 25.

One glaring omission in the present paper is the question of conscience. However, the primary importance of conscience and personal responsibility underlies practically all the considerations mentioned in the discussion.